FOCUS ON

First Certificate

TEACHER'S BOOK

SUE O'CONNELL

Nelson

Thomas Nelson and Sons Ltd
Nelson House Mayfield Road
Walton-on-Thames Surrey
KT12 5PL UK

51 York Place
Edinburgh
EH1 3JD UK

Thomas Nelson (Hong Kong) Ltd
Toppan Building 10/F
22A Westlands Road
Quarry Bay Hong Kong

© Sue O'Connell 1987

First published by HarperCollins Publishers 1987
Reprinted 1988, 1990 (twice), 1991
ISBN 0-00-370052-6

This edition first published by Thomas Nelson and Sons Ltd 1993
ISBN 0-17-556614-3
NPN 9 8 7 6 5 4 3 2

►Acknowledgements

The author and publishers are grateful to the University of
Cambridge Local Examinations Syndicate for their permission to
reproduce the information on page 9.

Contents

UNIT BY UNIT PLAN

	Reading texts	Grammar/Functions	Writing	Listening/Comm. activities	Study boxes/Exam practice
UNIT 1A	**Taking a break**				
Going places	1 I can't travel without … *p. 2* 2 Dear travel agent *p. 3*	1 Relative clauses *p. 5 (Text 1)* 2 Review of present tenses *p. 10* Likes & dislikes/preferences *p. 1* Expressing need & use *p. 7*	Directed writing – holiday ads/choices *p. 12*	📼1 Hotels *p. 9* 📼2 Suitcases *p. 11* CA1 I can't travel without … *p. 2* CA2 Game *p. 7*	1 Catch (phrasal verbs) *p. 4* 2 Live (phrasal verbs) *p. 6* 3 Adjectives + prepositions *p. 9* Vocabulary review *p. 14*
UNIT 2A	**Other people's jobs**				
Lifestyles	1 Waiter for a week *p. 19* 2 Traffic wardens *p. 24*	1 Adjectives & adverbs *p. 17* 2 Simple past *p. 21* 3 Past continuous *p. 25* Disagreeing *p. 16*	Informal letter *p. 28*	📼1 Job opportunities *p. 21* 📼2 A life at sea *p. 27* CA Working can be a health hazard *p. 23*	1 The use of articles 1 *p. 18* 2 Do & make *p. 23* 3 Put (phrasal verbs) *p. 27* Vocabulary review *p. 29*
UNIT 3A	**Enthusiasms**				
Personal concerns	1 Personal preferences *p. 31* 2 A new way to jump *p. 39*	1 Present perfect simple *p. 33 (Text 1)* 2 Present perfect continuous *p. 37 (FL1)* 3 Modal verbs: ability *p. 43*	1 Speeches *p. 35* 2 Directed writing – book choices *p. 44*	📼1 Hobbies *p. 35 (Text 1)* 📼2 The Bristol run *p. 42* CA 20 questions *p. 41*	1 The opposite of/opposite to *p. 37* Verb + preposition *p. 37* 2 Adjectives with numbers *p. 38* 3 Order of adjectives *p. 42* Vocabulary review *p. 45*
UNIT 4A	**Lawbreakers**				
An element of risk	1 Seven banks a day are robbed in LA *p. 47* 2 You're already well equipped to prevent crime *p. 50* 3 Granny, 70, holds up a bank! *p. 54*	1 Modal verbs: obligation *p. 48* 2 Participles *p. 55 (Texts 1, 2, 3)* Describing clothes *p. 51, p. 55* Describing people *p. 55*	1 Speech *p. 49 (LI)* 2 Description *p. 57*	📼1 Crime report *p. 50* 📼2 Bad start to a honeymoon *p. 53* CA Witness *p. 52*	1 Rob vs. steal *p. 46* 2 Get (phrasal verbs) 1 *p. 52* 3 Break (phrasal verbs) *p. 54* 4 Compound adjectives *p. 55* Vocabulary review *p. 58*
UNIT 5A	**Waste not, want not**				
The world we live in	1 One-trip living *p. 59* 2 Recycling *p. 64* 3 Friends of the Earth *p. 66*	1 Conditional 1 *p. 61* 2 Conditional 2 *p. 66 (Text 3)* 3 Modal verbs: permission *p. 70* Cause/result, addition, concession *p. 67*	Discussion *p. 67 (CA1)*	📼1 The sweet, short life of products *p. 62* 📼2 National parks *p. 69* CA1 Spot the difference (pollution) *p. 63* CA2 The Country Code *p. 68*	1 Wear (phrasal verbs) *p. 63* 2 Plural-form nouns *p. 65* 3 Set (phrasal verbs) *p. 71* Vocabulary review *p. 72*
UNIT 6A	**The shape of things to come**				
Changes	1 The robot wine waiter *p. 75* 2 The £100 car telephone *p. 79*	1 Talking about the future 1 *p. 74* 2 Sudden decisions, offers, suggestions, threats *p. 78* 3 Talking about the future 2 *p. 81 (FL2)* Expressing sequence *p. 78*	1 Instructions *p. 77 (FL1)* 2 Description/discussion *p. 84 (FL2)*	📼1 Word processor mishaps *p. 77* 📼2 The year 2000 *p. 81* CA1 Role play – Selling a car phone *p. 80 (Text 2)* CA2 Describe & draw *p. 84*	1 Let (phrasal verbs) *p. 80* 2 Cut (phrasal verbs) *p. 84* Vocabulary review *p. 85*

Cross-references to related sections are given in brackets.
KEY: CA = Communication activity   FL = Focus on listening   LI = Lead-in

INTRODUCTION

Focus on First Certificate is a complete, integrated course which practises all the skills needed to pass the five papers of the *Cambridge First Certificate in English* examination. The new edition, which is in full colour, contains all the original material together with a new writing reference section (the Writing Bank), and many new illustrations.

The material has been chosen to represent as wide a range of contemporary written and spoken English as possible. Texts come from newspapers, both quality and popular, from magazines, advertisements, information leaflets and non-fiction writing of all kinds. The recordings include informal conversations, interviews with adults and children, a lecture, a monologue and various radio consumer and magazine programmes. All the reading texts and a proportion of the listening texts are authentic, as in the examination itself.

The questions, exercises and activities based on this material include the full range of examination-format questions – multiple-choice, true/false, table completion and so on – but are not restricted to these alone. The aim has been to provide a balance between skills development work which is genuinely motivating and the necessary but narrower examination practice.

Focus on First Certificate also includes full grammar coverage, graded writing practice and a very wide variety of communication activities, reflecting the emphasis which the examination gives to oral/aural ability. Special features are the **Study Boxes**, the **Exam Practice** material, the **Functions Bank** and the **Writing Bank**, all of which are described below.

Vocabulary and grammar from the texts, the grammar sections and the Study Boxes are systematically revised in the Vocabulary review sections and in Exam Practice A.

HOW TO USE THE COURSE

The course is divided into six broad topic areas, each comprising two units (A and B) which are linked thematically. Units 1A–6A are followed by Units 1B–6B in the Student's Book.

There are two possible ways of working through the course, and a decision between them will depend on the type of course in question.

- *Sequential* (Units 1A–6A followed by Units 1B–6B) – more suited to a long-term part-time course (for example, 4 hours per week for 30 weeks).
- *Zig-zag* (Unit 1A followed by Unit 1B and so on) – more suited to a short-term intensive course (for example, 15–20 hours per week for three months).

The B units revise and extend the grammar and skills practised in previous A units. Thus, on a long-term course, returning to the B units at the mid-way point will serve to recycle items introduced some considerable time earlier. On a short-term course, on the other hand, the juxtaposition of units will have greater impact, will serve to consolidate what has been recently learned, and will provide exam training at an earlier stage in the course.

Each unit covers all five papers of the exam, but different weight is given to the various skills in different units. For example, informal letter writing is introduced in detail in Unit 2A and recycled in Unit 2B. In general, the A units include more detailed guidance in the skills than the B units.

Each unit has an 'umbrella' topic and contains materials relating to several loosely-linked sub-topics. For example, Unit 3B: Looking After Yourself covers diet, food, exercise and First Aid.

The unit by unit plan at the beginning of this book shows the total content of each unit in the Student's Book, with page references. Italicised elements in brackets refer to other sections in a unit that relate closely. *Note*: This interrelationship should be noted if a teacher plans to adopt a different order of presentation in a unit.

The time needed to work through a unit will vary according to the amount of class time spent on materials and activities, and the amount set for homework. As a general rule, a unit will take a minimum of 6 hours, and the whole course is likely to occupy 80–120 teaching hours.

Exam practice B provides six practice papers in the Use of English. These have been designed to revise language covered in each A/B pair of units and so can usefully be introduced after each of the six B units, whichever method of progress through the book has been chosen.

Exam practice C provides six practice 'thematic packages' for the Interview. These have been linked to topics in the book and can either be introduced following the appropriate units or reserved for more intensive examination practice towards the end of the course.

The Functions Bank can be used for the presentation of functional language or for students' reference before, during or after communication activities. Page references to the Functions Bank are given throughout the book.

The *Writing Bank* provides models for each of the writing formats together with notes on layout and organisation, examples of useful language, and topics for further practice. It can be used for class study when a particular format is first introduced, and students should be encouraged to make full use of it for reference and revision when they tackle similar writing tasks later. Page references to the Writing Bank are given throughout the book.

There is a detailed *Index* of structures and functions at the end of the book.

A NOTE ON THE TEACHING APPROACH

The examination's emphasis on communicative ability is reflected in the methodology underlying this course. In addition to the communication activities, many other exercises and tasks suggest that students collaborate by pooling their ideas or comparing their answers. Clearly, this will only be useful if students use English to communicate!

If your students are not used to this method of working, and if they share a first language, it would be helpful to explain the purpose of the student-centred activities to them at the start of the course. Though they will probably find communicating in English frustrating at first, if they are willing to co-operate and persevere, they will notice a steady improvement in fluency and communicative ability. The long-term benefits will be well worth the initial difficulties.

NOTES ON INDIVIDUAL SECTIONS

Lead-in

The aim of the lead-in sections is threefold: firstly to stimulate interest in a topic; secondly to involve students at a personal level, and thirdly to revise and extend topic vocabulary.

A wide variety of tasks and activities is used, including quizzes and questionnaires, matching pictures and headlines to texts and spotting deliberate mistakes. All involve an element of student-centred work and the communication of personal choices or opinions to a partner or group. In this respect, the lead-in activities also serve to practise the skills and techniques needed in the oral part of the *First Certificate* examination.

In general, these preliminary tasks and discussions provide a very important jumping-off point for each unit. They draw on what experience students already have of a topic and involve the exchange of opinions and the pooling of information and language. By making a personal contribution in this way, students embark on the unit with a sense of achievement and are more motivated to continue.

Reading texts

The 28 reading texts come from a wide variety of sources including newspapers and magazine articles, advertisements and modern travel writing. They vary in length, style and intention and, wherever possible, appear in their original format.

In most cases, texts have pre-questions to provide a reason for reading and to practise the skills of skimming and scanning. Students' attention should always be drawn to these beforehand, and comprehension of the questions themselves should be checked.

There is a wide range of follow-up exercises. 14 of the 28 texts have multiple-choice questions in the examination style. Other exercises include true/false, sequencing and open completion comprehension questions. The vocabulary-matching exercises and other vocabulary tasks are designed to encourage students to make logical deductions about the meanings of unknown words and so increase their confidence in reading authentic material.

The exercises have been designed to highlight key vocabulary and structural items and, in general, it is not advisable to cover additional vocabulary in too much detail. In fact, too much attention given to the meanings of unknown words can be discouraging and counter-productive in that it emphasises what students do **not** know, rather than what they do. This approach can also detract from overall understanding and spoil students' enjoyment of a reading task.

A selection of vocabulary from the texts in each unit is revised in the Vocabulary review sections at the end. These items are listed in the Teacher's Notes in order to enable teachers to give them adequate attention.

Focus on grammar

Each unit has either two or three grammar sections and these cover all the main areas tested in the *First Certificate* exam. It is assumed that students will already have met most of this grammar during the course of their studies, and so the grammar sections here are designed to review and summarise the key points, and to provide practice and revision exercises.

Study boxes

There are from two to four Study Boxes in each unit, usually relating to language which is used in the reading or listening texts. These isolate a number of language items which are frequently tested in the examination and which students should make a special point of learning. Areas covered include dependent prepositions and prepositional phrases, compound adjectives and the order of adjectives, phrasal verbs and use of articles.

Items from the Study Boxes are tested in the Vocabulary review and Exam practice A sections at the end of units.

Focus on listening

There are 24 listening texts and these are recorded on two accompanying cassettes, which remain the same for the New Edition. The tapescripts are reproduced at the end of this book.

The recordings represent a mixture of scripted and authentic material, as is the case in the examination itself. They include a variety of speech situations, both formal and informal, and involve anything from one to seven speakers of all ages.

The questions reflect the full range of those used in the examination: multiple-choice, true/false, blank-filling, selection and so on. Time should always be allowed for students to read through the instructions and question(s), and their understanding of these should be checked. Each recording should be played through twice, without pauses.

In checking answers to the questions, useful vocabulary, idioms and other language points can be highlighted.

Focus on writing

These sections cover all the kinds of writing required in Paper 2 (Composition) and Paper 3, Section B (Directed Writing). They are supplemented by the reference material and further practice in the Writing Bank.

Each of the main composition topics (letter, descriptive, narrative, discursive and speech) is introduced and its key features focused on. Later units recycle these topics and, in the last unit, 6B, example questions for all five topics are given as final revision.

Throughout the course, emphasis is placed on the importance of planning written work, and many of the writing sections include activities in which students prepare in groups prior to the writing stage.

Communication activities

The communication activities provide practice for the Interview in the examination. They include games and role plays, quizzes, brain teasers, 'spot the difference' and 'describe and draw' activities. Overall, there is a balance between activities where students compete to achieve a goal, and ones where they co-operate.

The aim of these activities is the freer, more creative use of language, with the emphasis on *communication* rather than on accuracy. Many include references to the Functions Bank and this can be used by students before an activity for initial practice or referred to during an activity. (*Note*: Students should be discouraged from leaving their books open at the Functions Bank or referring to it too much, since communication will inevitably be less spontaneous and fluent as a result.) An additional way of using the Functions Bank is to direct students to it after an activity so that they can check the available language and make a note of expressions which they have not used, to be borne in mind for the future.

The Teacher's Notes give guidance in preparing students for the activities, in monitoring their work and in following up afterwards. In general, once the necessary preparation has taken place (including any changes in seating arrangements), students should be able to carry on without further assistance from the teacher. On-the-spot correction, however tempting, is not advisable, though notes of major or recurring mistakes can be made for dealing with at a later stage.

For those activities which involve an 'information gap' element, individual notes for participants are usually given in the end section of the Student's Book. Page references direct students to the correct place to turn to, and they should **not** look at each other's information!

Vocabulary review/Exam practice A

There is a Vocabulary review section containing 15 multiple-choice questions at the end of each of the A units. The B units finish with an Exam practice A section with 25 multiple-choice questions, as in Paper 1 of the examination.

In all cases, the correct answer comes from one of the texts, from a Study Box or from a grammar section in the unit in question or from a preceding unit. References to the source of these items are given in the Teacher's Notes so that students can be reminded of the original contexts.

In addition, two units have an 'odd man out' exercise. These do not occur in the examination but serve to review an area of topic vocabulary very effectively.

As in the *First Certificate* examination, all the vocabulary in the Vocabulary review sections and Exam practice A sections falls within the scope of Level 5 of the *Cambridge English Lexicon*: Hindmarsh (CUP).

Exam practice B

This contains six practice papers for Paper 3 (Use of English) Section A. The exercises represent the full range of those which occur in the exam, and the only difference is that each practice paper contains **two** cloze tests (Question 1) rather than one as in the exam. For exam practice purposes, students should be asked to work through **either** Question 1a **or** Question 1b together with the other questions in a time allowance of 1 to 1¼ hours.

Each practice paper is linked to an A/B pair of units, and many of the questions revise grammar points which have been covered in these or preceding units. Specific references to such coverage is given, where useful, in the Teacher's Notes. Material from the Exam practice B section can be used at any stage of the course or reserved for exam preparation towards the end of the course.

Exam practice C

This contains six complete 'thematic packages' for Paper 5 (Interview). These too have been linked to topics in the book and can either be introduced following the appropriate unit or reserved for more intensive exam practice in the later stages of the course.

THE REQUIREMENTS OF THE EXAM

PAPER 1   Reading Comprehension (1 hour)   40 marks

A 25 multiple-choice questions designed to test vocabulary and formal grammatical control, in sentence contexts.

B 15 multiple-choice questions based on three or more texts, designed to test comprehension of gist or detailed content.

(The initial mark weighting in Section A is one mark, and in Section B two marks, for each item.)

PAPER 2   Composition (1½ hours)   40 marks

Two compositions from a choice of descriptive, narrative or discursive topics, including one based on a choice of set books.

Assessment is based on organisation and clarity of content, accuracy of grammatical control, fluency and range of expression.

PAPER 3   Use of English (2 hours)   40 marks

A Open-completion or transformation items designed to test active control of the language at an appropriate communicative level.

B Directed writing exercise to test ability to interpret and present information.

PAPER 4   Listening Comprehension
(approx. 30 minutes)   20 marks

Questions of varying type (selection, re-ordering, blank-filling etc.) to test accurate understanding of spoken English, based on recorded material.

PAPER 5   Interview
(approx. 15 minutes)   40 marks

Based on a picture stimulus, and related passages and other material. The interview may, optionally, be based partly on a choice of set books and be conducted, also optionally, with individual candidates or in groups of two or three.

Assessment is based on fluency, grammatical accuracy, pronunciation (individual sounds, and stress and linking of phrases), communicative ability and vocabulary.

UNIT NOTES AND KEY

UNIT 1A Taking a break

▶Lead-in (p. 1)

Before students open their books, introduce the topic orally. For example, ask students to work in pairs to find out about each other's last holiday. Then each student should report back briefly on what their partner has told them.

First ask students to identify the types of holiday shown in the pictures: **A** skiing/winter sports; **B** camping; **C** mountain walking/hiking; **D** sightseeing/cultural; **E** beach/seaside; **F** sailing; **G** cruise; **H** safari.

You could also introduce some topic vocabulary at this stage, but it's best to keep the introduction fairly brief.

1 As students do the first task, emphasise that money is no object!
2 While students work in pairs on the second task, it's useful to monitor and note particular errors and language needs.
3 Instead of referring students to the Functions Bank, you may prefer to present the relevant language on the board and practise it orally.

Vocabulary included in the Vocabulary review: can't bear, keen on (Functions Bank).

▶Text 1 · I can't travel without ... (p. 2)

As an introduction, ask students to describe the picture and discuss what kind of person it represents.

a Richard Branson ('travelling light')
b Mel Calman ('keep a diary')
c Frank Muir ('penknife ... I have never used it')
d Patrick Lichfield (correspondence); Mel Calman (sketch book). Also possibly Richard Branson (notebooks).
e Barry Norman (credit card); Mel Calman (new diary)

Note: Students who finish quickly can check their answers together.

Vocabulary included in the Vocabulary review: do without (line 1), catch up with (column 1, line 7; see also Study Box 1), filling with (column 2, line 3), except (column 2, line 14), at a moment's notice (column 4, line 12).

▶Communication activity 1 (p. 2)

The clearest way to set up this activity is to give students the name of a suitable object (such as an alarm clock) and then ask them questions until you 'guess' the answer. You may want to practise some question forms first if necessary.

Make sure everyone has chosen an object before pairwork begins. Again, students can report back on their partner's chosen object at the end.

▶Text 2 · Dear travel agent ... (p. 3)

2 Pre-questions

a At a gite in France.
b The story is an example of a silly or unreasonable complaint about a holiday.

3 True/false

a False. ('petty, silly little things')
b True. ('fails to live up to the brochure promises')
c True. ('baby minding')
d True. ('an initial complaint')
e False. ('eventually')
f True. ('self-catering')
g False. ('she was angry')
h True. ('do their research')
i True. ('sort it out there and then')
j False. (only those who have complained and are 'unhappy with the response')

4 Vocabulary matching

a deluge
b petty
c package
d cots
e practically non-existent
f issued a summons
g met in full
h furious
i hurricane
j conciliation facilities

7 Language check: prepositions

a as; with
b in
c of; under
d for
e On
f up
g In; of
h along; with
i as
j about

▶Focus on grammar 1 · Relative clauses (p. 5)

Exercise 1

a defining
b non-defining
c non-defining
d defining

Exercise 2

1 f who/that
2 e which/that
3 g that
4 a who/that
5 d whose
6 i which/that
7 j that
8 c which/that
9 h whose
10 b which/that

The relative pronoun can be omitted from sentences 3, 6, 7, 8, and 10.

Exercise 3

a The house (*that*) we used to live in has just been sold.
b The old lady *who* lives across the road has got eight cats.
c The friend (*who/that*) you were looking for has just come in.
d The old chair (*which/that*) my grandmother left me is worth a fortune.
e I bought my watch at a shop *whose* name I can't remember.
f The writer *whose* latest book was published on Tuesday lives in New York.
g The neighbour *who* has been to Sao Paulo says he's never seen anything like it.
h The blouse (*which/that*) I gave Helen for her birthday is worn out already.
i The student *who* came top in Maths at school has gone to university.
j None of the people (*who/that*) went to Paris this spring complained about the hotel.

Exercise 4 (Example answers)

a ... *which* (is famous for its tennis tournament)
b ... *which* (are to be held in ...)
c ... *whose* (name is ...)
d ... *who* (reached the New World in 1492.)
e ... *which* (is in the Himalayas)

Exercise 5

Commas are needed in sentences *b*, *d* and *g*. The relative pronoun can be omitted in sentences *c* and *f*.

▶Communication activity 2 (p. 7)

1 Vocabulary and definitions

You may prefer your students to keep their books closed while you cover this preparatory section. In this case, choose suitable examples of objects (such as *pen, microscope, saw, key, clothes*) and elicit from students the various ways of defining them.

The practice activities in *b* and *c* can both be done in pairs or groups.

2 Game

Preparation

Equipment: It will save time if you are able to prepare the three sets of paper for each group in advance. If this is not possible, ask each group to read the instructions and to prepare their own slips beforehand. Check that these are correct before proceeding.

Note: It is helpful if the numbers and letters are written on different colours of paper (or in a different colour ink) so that they can be easily distinguished.

Language: Again, you may prefer to present a selection of useful language on the board and practise it, rather than refer students to the Functions Bank at this stage.

Procedure

Ideally, students should be grouped in small circles round tables. Even if desks are fixed, however, it is usually possible to move chairs so that this arrangement is achieved.

Tell students to pick a slip in order to decide which holiday they're going on. Ask them to decide specific details: **where** it is, **when** it is, and for **how long**.

Ask them to read through the instructions, and check that these are understood.

Once the game has started, make sure each group is playing according to the rules and scoring correctly.

Encourage players to ask questions and to challenge each other.

Discourage too much argument! Some students may feel they mustn't allow any points, however justified!

Note any language errors and gaps for attention later.

Feedback

Ask groups to report back on the results of their games. Deal with any important language problems.

▶ Focus on listening 1 (p. 9)

| 1 The Atlantic | 2 The Plaza |
| 3 The Concord | 4 The Royal |

5 Days: Fridays and Tuesdays
6 Time: Third week in July
7 Price: From £159 to £191
8 Insurance: The most expensive: £14.25
    The cheapest: £10.80

Check/recap by asking students to describe the buildings orally. (They could also do this in writing as consolidation.)

Useful vocabulary: look through, pick up, end up; three-storey building, terrace, the rear; curved, situated, steps (versus stairs); to screen . . . from; a (steep) slope, balconies, break up (of schools).

▶ Focus on grammar 2 · Review of the present tenses (p. 10)

Exercise 1

a The kettle is boiling; Water boils
b I'm living; I live
c He plays; He's playing
d it's raining; it rains
e We usually bath; the children are bathing

The present simple
The following are examples:
1 *a* wins
  b falls
2   stops

The present continuous
1 *a* The telephone's ringing
  b I'm working
2   we're . . . going/travelling

Exercise 2

a I'm looking	*f* I see
b he has	*g* you think
c He's thinking	*h* are you seeing
d This jug holds	*i* My parents are having
e You look	*j* Who's holding

Exercise 3

a What are you doing; We're spending
b Oil and water do not mix; Oil floats
c Why are you cooking; You know; Helen only eats
d I don't understand; he's saying; Is he speaking
e I normally go; I'm working
f I know; you mean; I don't agree
g I do; he cooks; we both give

▶ Focus on listening 2 (p. 11)

1 Vocabulary check
lock, label, handle, catch, buckle, zip, strap, padlock

2 1 expensive and heavy
   2 toughness (strength)
   3 to get damaged
   4

	Riviera	Windsor	Tornado	Mayfair
a Length	67cm	68cm	75cm	80cm
b Material (see below)	PVC	nylon	ABS	aluminium
c Fastening/Security	zip+padlock	catches	2 locks	2 locks
d Number of wheels	4	2	2	2
e Strap or Handle for pushing/pulling	strap	strap	handle	handle
f Price	£67	£32.50	£109.50	£199
g Tester's verdict	good value for money	good value but material might get torn	strong but heavy	smart and practical but overpriced

▶ Focus on writing · Directed writing (p. 12)

1 *a* A, C	*e* C, B
b A, D, E	*f* F, E
c B, D, F	*g* C
d F, D	

2 Encourage students to study the information carefully before they begin, and to make notes so they can include all the relevant points.

Tell them to use their own words where possible rather than quote from the texts throughout.

The answers given below are not the only 'right' ones, and other choices are possible if well enough argued.

a Ballard: **Narracott** (parties and competitions to keep the children amused; an indoor pool for Tom; dancing and discos for Susan; free sports facilities for their parents; reasonable prices).

b Fellows: **Lundy Island** (by the sea; no cars, silence and space; small hotel, self-catering for economy). *Note: Not* Trevose House (no children under 10).

c Gilchrist: **McConnell's** (hotel with traditional hospitality including Christmas carols. Unlikely to be too many children). *Note: Not* Invercauld (half price for children).

d Brown: **Mon Ami** (plenty of entertainment, baby/radio listening devices in rooms; lift for Dick's mother).

▶Vocabulary review (p. 14)

Text and line numbers are given in brackets.

1 *d* (1. Mel Calman)
2 *b* (1. Mel Calman)
3 *c* (Writing)
4 *a* (1. Barry Norman)
5 *d* (2.8)
6 *c* (Listening 2)
7 *d* (Writing)
8 *b* (Functions)

9 *a* (Functions)
10 *c* (2.53)
11 *c* (1. Patrick Lichfield)
12 *a* (2.53/54)
13 *b* (2.19)
14 *d* (1)
15 *b* (2.17)

UNIT **2A** Other people's jobs

▶Lead-in 1 (p. 15)

Ask students to work together to identify the ten jobs as quickly as possible (5 minutes) and check their answers. Check relevant vocabulary for equipment too at this stage.

1 carpenter (hammer, nails); 2 librarian (Note: bookshop v. library); 3 fireman (helmet, hose); 4 film director; 5 painter (paint brush, tin of paint); 6 dustman (dustbin); 7 hairdresser (scissors, brush, comb); 8 architect/draughtsman (drawing board); 9 mechanic/engineer (spanner); 10 dentist (dentist's surgery chair).

Allow students a few moments to think about the questions before they discuss the answers in pairs or small groups. Tell them they **must** finally agree on one job for each category and be prepared to give reasons for their choice.

Monitor the discussions and notice errors and language needs, particularly in the area of comparatives and superlatives (Focus on grammar 1).

▶Lead-in 2 (p. 15)

1 Check that students understand the introduction and what they have to do. Don't refer them to the table on page 16 at this stage.

After sufficient reading and discussion time, invite possible answers and ask students to say which words or phrases helped them to guess the jobs. Don't confirm or deny any of the suggestions yet.

2 Refer students to the table on page 16 and, when this has been considered, confirm final answers:

Place	Extract	Job
Photographic Studio	C	Male model
Museum	B	Museum attendant
Restaurant	D	Waiter
Holiday Resort	A	Holiday representative

3 Ask students to compare their answers when they have finished this exercise. Again, ask them to justify their answers by saying which words or phrases helped them.

a D (apron, valet's jacket), (C)
b D (the place is jumping, etc.)
c C (agony of indecision, embarrassment)
d A (broken tap, lost wallet), (B)
e B (I saw my life ticking by)
f D (the thrill of a film star)
g A (Alan)

4 **Discussion points**

b Ask students to report back briefly on their discussions.

5 **Disagreeing**

Practise the language in the table and examples orally, with attention to stress and intonation, before students start pair work.

6 This can be an optional writing exercise. Ask students to answer the questions in 150–200 words.

Vocabulary included in the Vocabulary review: a while (extract A), interest *in* (extract C).

▶ Focus on grammar 1 · Adjectives and adverbs (p. 17)

Exercise 1

1 carefully	8 modern
2 terribly	9 previous
3 nervous	10 helpfully
4 loud	11 firmly
5 quickly	12 unfortunately
6 complete	13 closely
7 confident	14 straight

Exercise 2

a the most stressful	*f* more annoying
b more useful	*g* the least sociable
c more carefully	*h* harder
d more quietly	*i* the worst
e fitter	*j* the most expensive

▶ Text 1 · Waiter for a week (p. 19)

Pre-questions – suggested answers

a Fetching orders, helping to serve, clearing tables etc.
b The long hours.
c The distance of the restaurant from the kitchen.
d The way they called him or ignored him.

1 Vocabulary

1 *b*	5 *b*
2 *a*	6 *c*
3 *c*	7 *c*
4 *a*	

2 True/false

a False. (It's the senior waiter's responsibility.)
b False. (They share the tips equally.)
c True. ('What can you do …?')
d False. ('The commis then comes up …')
e True. (yelling, banging, hissing).
f True. ('You need … to stay out of trouble.')
g False. ('Deference, a quality I usually lack.')
h True.

Discussion points

For variety, section A points can be discussed by the class as a whole and section B by the students in small groups.

Vocabulary included in the Vocabulary review: work as a *team* (line 3), although (7), responsible for (10), wrist (39), treat (48).

▶ Focus on listening 1 (p. 21)

1 *a* Cost: free.
  b Young Engineer of the Year Competition: closing date end of May; prize: £1,000.

TAUNTON
Job Description Trainee sales person
Number of Vacancies 1 Part Time ☐
Full Time ☑
Wages/Salary £3,000 a year
Age 16-18
Additional Information driving licence needed

WELLS
Job Description Groom
Number of Vacancies 2 Part Time ☐
Full Time ☑
Wages/Salary £40 a week
Age Open
Additional Information Experience is necessary

WARMLEY
Job Description Shop assistant
Number of Vacancies 20 Part Time ☑
Full Time ☑
Wages/Salary £2 an hour
Age Over 16 —
Additional Information

EASTON
Job Description Trainee baker
Number of Vacancies 1 Part Time ☐
Full Time ☑
Wages/Salary £55-£65 a week
Age Open
Additional Information must start at 6 a.m.

▶ Focus on grammar 2 · The simple past (p. 21)

Exercise 1

1 in	6 when
2 during	7 until
3 ago	8 after
4 at	9 before
5 for	10 on

Exercise 2 (Example answers)

1 … hated taking examinations.
2 … sent him to bed.
3 … rarely travelled abroad.
4 … I played a lot of tennis.
5 … did you like best?

2 Irregular verbs

Infinitive	Past	Past Participle
become	became	become
bite	bit	bitten
break	broke	broken
catch	caught	caught
choose	chose	chosen
cost	cost	cost
drive	drove	driven
fall	fell	fallen
feel	felt	felt
fly	flew	flown
hear	heard	heard
lay	laid	laid
lose	lost	lost
put	put	put
ride	rode	ridden
shoot	shot	shot
steal	stole	stolen
teach	taught	taught
tear	tore	torn
write	wrote	written

▶ Communication activity · Working can be a health hazard (p. 23)

Introduction

You may prefer to introduce the subject of stress orally, rather than by reading through the text on page 23. The main points to be covered in a discussion are:

What is stress? What causes it? (danger, pressure of work, frustration)

What jobs have high stress? Which have low stress? (avoiding examples on the list, if possible)

What are the results of stress? How can we overcome stress?

The task

Check that students understand the instructions and that they know all the jobs on the list. Ask one student in each pair to be responsible for drawing up the three groups of jobs on a separate piece of paper. Emphasise that they must agree on their groups and be prepared to say **why** they have put particular jobs in particular groups.

Set a time limit of 10 minutes for the activity, and monitor progress.

As pairs finish, ask them to compare their results briefly with those of other pairs. Check that they have remembered to select a job with the highest stress and one with the lowest.

Feedback

Check first on students' choices of highest-stress and lowest-stress jobs, asking them to give reasons. Allow other students to disagree or challenge.

Then ask each pair to suggest one other high-stress job on their list, and one low-stress job, giving reasons. Discuss briefly.

Finally refer students to the official results on page 217 of their book, and again discuss possible reasons for the high or low ranking of particular jobs – especially those which differ from the students' ranking.

Optional additional activity

This can be used to start or finish a lesson. Ask students in pairs to write down three people who:
– work with animals
– travel for their work
– work with their hands
– sometimes risk their lives in their work

▶ **Text 2** (p. 24)

Suggested lead-in

Ask students to suggest places where you are not allowed to park a car, for example on a pedestrian crossing, on a motorway, on double yellow lines (UK) etc. Ask what happens if you **do** park in these places.

Elicit: parking offence, parking ticket, parking meter, traffic warden, fine, to tow away, towing truck, clamp (an explanation of clamps will be needed).

Clarify meaning as necessary.

1 Scanning questions
  a Ahn Ong-Chul (Korea)
  b Sao Paulo
  c Rome
  d Rotterdam
  e Rome, Sao Paulo

Multiple-choice
  2 *d* (takes real pleasure in her work)
  3 *c* (pickpockets)
  4 *b* (11 hours a day, sub-zero temperatures)
  5 *c* (so many double- and triple-parked cars)
  6 *a* (world towing record)
  7 *d* (a driver once tried to run her down)

Vocabulary included in the Vocabulary review: fine, without + ing, *no matter* how hard, run (somebody) down, concentrate *on*.

▶ **Focus on grammar 3 · The past continuous** (p. 25)

Exercise 1 (Example answers)
  1 ... was enjoying herself on holiday.
  2 ... was having a bath.
  3 ... sold the house.
  4 ... broke in.
  5 ... was already working.
  6 ... had to walk or ride.
  7 ... pulled into the space.
  8 ... had a party to celebrate.
  9 ... were sunbathing in the garden.
  10 ... was waiting outside another.

Exercise 2

1 happened	11 was heading
2 was working	12 began
3 usually cycled	13 moved
4 was trying	14 went
5 was just beginning	15 came
6 left	16 was lying
7 thought	17 were standing
8 got	18 heard
9 cycled	19 sank
10 turned	20 arrived

▶ **Focus on listening 2 · A life at sea** (p. 27)

Introduction

Explain that students are going to hear an interview with a man who worked as a merchant seaman (explain what the merchant navy is, if necessary).

Ask students to read through the six statements in the first part, and the four multiple-choice questions in the second part. Check that there are no vocabulary problems in the questions. (*Note*: tell them that 'bellboy' will be explained during the recording.)

True/false
  1 False. ('it was an idea *I went along with*')
  2 False. (he wasn't needed)
  3 True. ('how to lay a table ... carry cups and saucers and plates ...')
  4 True. (difficult conditions, strict discipline)
  5 False. (he had to stand by the bellboard and wait for the bells to ring)
  6 False. (he never questioned what he was doing)

Multiple-choice
  7 *d* (six years plus four years)
  8 *b* (the living quarters were very poor – iron bunks, no carpets, etc.)
  9 *d* (the ship would have been smashed against the quay)
  10 *c* (he was finally convinced by people that it was time to leave)

▶ **Focus on writing · Informal letters** (p. 28)

Check that students' completed versions of the two tasks on page 28 are correct, since these will be used as models for the writing task which follows.

Check comprehension of the letter by asking, for example, why the writer is writing to Gill, and what changes there have been in his/her life.

Draw students' attention to the points in the list on page 29. This can be done before students actually turn to the list. For example, ask students to study the letter again briefly, and then to close their books. Ask what punctuation there was in the sender's address, how the letter began and ended, how the date was written, etc. Students can then turn to the notes for further details.

Note: It would be useful to have a brief revision of these points in a later lesson.

▶ **Vocabulary review** (p. 29)

1 *d* (2)	**9** *b* (1.10)
2 *d* (Lead-in, 2 C)	**10** *b* (1.3)
3 *c* (Lead-in, 2 A)	**11** *d* (Lead-in, 2C)
4 *b* (2, Michiko Demizu)	**12** *a* (1.48)
5 *c* (2, Elly van Driel)	**13** *c* (2, Marina Di Generoso)
6 *c* (Grammar 3)	**14** *b* (1.39)
7 *a* (2, Marina Di Generoso)	**15** *d* (1.7)
8 *a* (2, Michiko Demizu)	

UNIT **3A** Enthusiasms

▶**Lead-in** (p. 31)

You could introduce this activity by drawing two or three pieces of equipment connected with **your** hobby and asking students to guess what it is. This could lead to a brief class discussion about hobbies in general.

Tell students they don't need to put down the exact word for an item – a general word will do (for example, paints for artist's palette). Give them a few minutes to work on their own, and then ask them to compare their answers with a neighbour's and try to complete the rest.

Activity	Sewing	Gardening	Painting	Tennis	Cooking
Item 1	sewing machine	spade	(picture) frame	racket	saucepan
Item 2	cotton/ thread	(pot) plant	paints/ palette	net	scales
Item 3	scissors	(wellington) boots	paint brush	ball	knife
Item 4	needle	watering can	canvas/ easel	tennis shoes	whisk

▶**Text 1** (p. 31)

1 See whether any students can explain *windsurfing* and *budgerigar breeding* before they look at the key in the book. Ask them to read the descriptions of the four people and the clues to their hobbies. Check or teach *aggressive* and *aggressiveness*.

Ask students to guess what the four hobbies could be before they read the texts.

2 **A** Rosalind Plowright; **B** Geoff Capes; **C** Bill Sirs; **D** Sally Oppenheim. Ask students to explain how they decided on their answers.

3 **A** 'You can really get away from it all', 'a tremendous escape'.
   B 'The hobby gives me relaxation and peace of mind.'
   C 'It releases the tensions of work.'
   D 'When you're playing it, you can't think of anything else.'
   All four find their hobby a way of relaxing and escaping from the pressures of their work.

4 **Multiple-choice**
   Note: Students may well suggest additional or alternative answers.

   a A, C
   b C
   c B
   d A, C
   e D
   f A, D
   g B
   h A, C
   i B, D

   Again, ask students to say **how** they decided on their answers.

5 a exhilarating
   b claustrophobia
   c tensions
   d aggressiveness
   e frustration
   f elation

   Vocabulary included in the Vocabulary review: A: tend to (be), conscious of, keep fit; B: the opposite *of*, compete in; C: apart from + ing, approve of, in that case; D: *for* fun, score.

▶**Focus on grammar 1· The present perfect simple** (p. 33)

Exercise 1

   a since
   b for
   c for
   d since
   e since

Exercise 2

   a He's lost a lot of hair.
   b He's grown a moustache.
   c His eyesight has got worse.
   d He's put on weight.
   e He's changed his style of dress.

Exercise 3

   a Have you *ever* been to the opera?
   b Have they arrived *yet*?
   c She has *never* learned to drive.
   d I *still* haven't finished that book.
   e Your father hasn't phoned *yet*.

Exercise 4

   1 i
   2 h
   3 j
   4 g
   5 b
   6 d
   7 f
   8 a
   9 c
   10 e

▶**Focus on listening 1** (p. 35)

Revise *windsurfing*, *budgerigar breeding* and check *judo*.

Give students time to read through tasks 1 and 2 and answer any questions.

Activity	First Introduced	Made an Olympic Event		Costs	
Judo	1882	1964	Judo suit to buy	£ 15	
			Judo suit to hire	£5 a month	
Windsurfing	1969	1984	Beginner's board	£300	
			A racing board	£ 1,000	
Budgerigar Breeding	1840	✗	Price range for birds	£ 1 - £500	

2 a headquarters
   b March–September
   c dry suit
   d 01–127 3444
   e pink

▶**Focus on writing 1 · Speeches** (p. 35)

Exercise 1

1 You are the 'expert' for the moment (*a*) and you are talking to a group of say, 15 children, whom you've probably not met before (*b*). It's probably a fairly informal occasion and if your approach is too formal the children are likely to lose interest! (*c*) So, while you need to inform your audience, you also want to do it in an interesting and entertaining way (*d*).

2 You are talking to two or three friends, probably, (*a/b*) so it's definitely an informal occasion and a speech would be quite unsuitable! (*c*) You probably know something about your friends' likes and dislikes and also about the amount of money they are likely to be willing to spend (*b*). With this in mind, you want to offer clear advice and perhaps some encouragement as well (*d*).

3 Again you are talking to only two people but this time, although they're probably your age, you've only just met them (*a/b*). It's an informal occasion and you need to give clear information about the things you pass as you walk round **and** to make the people feel welcome and relaxed (*c/d*).

4 You are addressing a large number of people, including parents like you and teachers (*a/b*). It's definitely a formal occasion and a serious subject which you feel strongly about. You will need to speak very clearly and persuasively. Humour is probably not a good idea in the circumstances! (*c/d*)

   Note: You may like to set one of the above topics as a written exercise for additional practice.

Exercise 2 (True/false)

   a True
   b False
   c True
   d True
   e False
   f True
   g False

(There are no examples here, but phrasal verbs are a common feature in informal speech.)

Exercise 3 (Example answer)

OK, I'll show you how to poach an egg. Watch what I do. First of all you break the egg into a cup like this. You could use a saucer instead, if you like. (Be careful to pick out any pieces of shell.) Then you put about this much water into a shallow pan like this one and heat it. Don't put any vinegar or salt into the water, by the way – they make the white of the egg tough. When the water begins to boil gently, you can slide the egg into the pan like this – look. Now we'll let it cook for about three minutes. Another method is to take the pan off the heat, cover it and leave the egg to cook like that for 3½–4 minutes. Easy, isn't it?

Exercise 4

It is useful to have a preparation stage for this task during a class.

First check that students can answer the four questions on page 35 in relation to this speech situation.

Then ask students to make notes under the headings given in Notes 1. Check these notes before students begin the writing task. *Note*: Students could also work in pairs to discuss their notes, asking questions and making suggestions.

Go through the other notes on pages 36–7 and then set the task for homework.

Note: You may like to give the students the opportunity to deliver their speeches at a later date.

▶ Focus on grammar 2 . The present perfect continuous (p. 37)

Exercise 1 (Example answers)

a Because she's been crying.
b Because I've been running.
c Because he's been digging in the garden.
d Because I've been doing a lot of overtime.

Exercise 2

1 I've been sharing; came
2 left; applied; has been working
3 saw; have never read
4 have you been standing
5 have been; rejected
6 Have you heard; have announced; have been going out; thought
7 have you been doing; have seen; met
8 have been; have warned; have already occurred
9 haven't heard; wrote
10 have risen; joined

▶ Text 2 · A new way to jump (p. 39)

Introduction

Introduce the topic by asking what dangerous hobbies students can think of and whether they would be tempted to try any of them.

Pre-teach *parachute, harness, free fall*.

Ask students to speculate about what training for parachute jumping involves, how long it takes and how much it costs.

1 Pre-questions

a £385.
b About a day.
c Yes, very well.
d They enjoyed it and had no regrets.

2 True/false

a False. (They had saved towards a new car.)
b False. (She was so nervous that her hands were shaking.)
c True. (The gear proved 'surprisingly neat and easy to handle'.)
d True. (including a reserve)
e False. (Cathy jumped after David.)

f True. (They continued their free fall for longer and landed before Cathy.)
g True. (They both had a few seconds of free fall.)
h False. (It was a perfect landing.)
i False. (She had never been in an aeroplane.)

3 Vocabulary

a mock-up
b allayed their fears
c on its last legs
d posture
e blew it all
f navigate
g second nature
h in earnest

4 Multiple-choice

1 c ('They practised exits by sliding . . .')
2 b
3 b ('They detached themselves only when her parachute had opened safely.')
4 d ('it's just like putting the brakes on . . . ')

Discussion points

The discussion can be amongst the class as a whole, or in small groups.

Vocabulary included in the Vocabulary review: nervous (13), persuade (17), once (X has happened) (18), make up one's *mind* (18), to slide (33).

▶ Communication activity · 20 questions (p. 41)

Read through the instructions with the class and make sure they are understood.

Expand the list of possible questions, as suggested in the book, imagining that the activity in question is football.

Acting as Subject yourself, start the activity off. Choose a fairly easy hobby which students are likely to be able to guess without too much difficulty.

With a class which is larger than 16, it's probably best to divide students into two or more groups. Try to include a range of ability in each group.

Monitor the activity, but avoid interrupting if possible. Make it clear that everyone must listen out for mistakes in the questions, and that the Subject can only answer correct questions.

▶ Focus on listening 2 (p. 42)

Introduction

Discuss the difference between jogging and running (briefly) and the benefits (and possible dangers) of long-distance running.

Ask students to look carefully at the map of Bristol on page 42 and to locate:

the **City Centre**
Neptune's Statue
the **Hotel**
the **SS Great Britain**
Clifton Village
the **Suspension Bridge**

Ask them to read through the four multiple-choice questions (2–5).

Note: The listening text provides a number of examples of the language of describing directions, for example: I turned sharp left; I took the first turning on the left.

The most useful way of checking task 1 is to ask students to describe exactly what directions the runner took.

Multiple-choice

2 b (He doesn't *carry any money on him*; the 2p fee prevented him from crossing.)
3 b (It had a production of the 'Sound of Music'.)
4 a (He set out to run 5 miles and did so.)
5 c ('even if it is hilly').

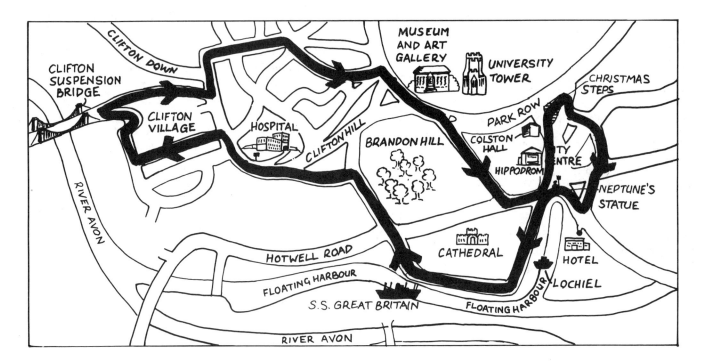

Additional activities

Here are some suggestions for further practice in giving and following directions:

1 Students study the Functions Bank on page 211.
2 Using the map of Bristol, students work in pairs. Student A decides on a starting point and destination, and a route between them. S/he gives Student B the starting point and then gives directions without mentioning the destination. Student B follows the directions and sees where s/he ends up!

   Note: It is best if A cannot see B's map for this activity.

3 Using a different map, students again work in pairs and reverse roles for the same activity.

▶ Focus on grammar 3 · Modal verbs 1: ability (p. 43)

Exercise 1

a could; can	*f* haven't been able to
b will never be able to	*g* was able to
c could; was able to	*h* couldn't
d could have	*i* I'll be able to
e Can	*j* was able to

▶ Focus on writing 2 · Directed writing (p. 44)

It is not advisable to treat all the written information in this section as a reading comprehension exercise. In many ways that would defeat the purpose of the task, which is to skim read the information and then scan for relevant detail. It is not necessary to understand every word in order to perform the required task, and students should be reassured on this point.

Suggested procedure

After students have read the instructions, ask them to read the information about the four family members. Check understanding as necessary.

Ask students to work in pairs and decide on suitable books for the four people. Once this has been done, they should underline any information in the descriptions of the books which they think is relevant.

Check the information that has been underlined with the class as a whole.

Ask students individually to make notes for the four paragraphs.

Check these on an individual basis.

Set the final paragraph writing task for homework. Alternatively, if you feel the class needs more guidance at this stage, build up the first paragraph on the board, with the help of students' suggestions, and then set the remaining three paragraphs as homework.

Example paragraphs

Jim would probably be pleased to receive *Computing Day By Day*. As he's recently bought a home computer, he's likely to have a lot to learn about using it still. The diary will give him useful information, and it will also enable him to make a note of things he's promised to do, so that he doesn't forget them in future!

I think Freda would enjoy either *Do It Yourself!* or *Houseplants through the Year*. The first would be a great help when Freda redecorates the lounge, since it has information about painting and wallcoverings, and also gives instructions for DIY jobs. The second would solve her problem of not having a garden, as it gives practical advice on growing houseplants.

I'd suggest giving Susan *Success in Writing and Study* because it has information about written work and studying which will be useful to her as she prepares for her 'A' Level examinations. There are also sections on application forms and on listening and note-taking which would be helpful when she applies to a teacher training college later.

The present I'd recommend for Tony would be *Nature Watchers*. It has a large number of colour photographs which should appeal to him, and the descriptions of people who work with animals might well give him ideas for other careers apart from that of being a vet. Finally, the advice on nature watching should be interesting and helpful for him.

▶ Vocabulary review (p. 45)

1 *c* (1.D)		**9** *c* (1.B)	
2 *a* (1.A)		**10** *b* (1.C)	
3 *d* (1.A)		**11** *a* (1.C)	
4 *a* (1.D)		**12** *d* (2.13)	
5 *b* (1.C)		**13** *b* (2.18)	
6 *b* (2.18)		**14** *a* (2.33)	
7 *d* (1.C)		**15** *d* (2.17)	
8 *c* (1.B)			

UNIT **4A** Lawbreakers

▶Lead-in (p. 46)

Ask students to look at the picture briefly and then to read the text. Check that they understand the situation and instructions fully by asking questions like:

- *a* Is anyone at home in either of the houses? (Answer: No.)
- *b* Where are the family who live at No. 37? (Answer: They're on holiday.)
- *c* Does the car belong to the family from No. 37? (Answer: No, it belongs to the visitors at No. 35.)
- *d* What do you have to do now? (Answer: Find ten things that would invite a burglar to call.)

The activity is best done in pairs, so that students can help each other. If they work individually, it is best to set a time limit of, say, five minutes and then ask them to compare their answers with their neighbour's.

Ask students to report back the points they have found and to explain why they could be invitations to burglars. The full list is as follows:

1 In No. 35, downstairs window open – useful for the cat **and** the burglar.
2 Upstairs window left open near a drainpipe and a flat roof – makes it easy for the burglar to enter.
3 Luggage left on the roof-rack of the car at No. 37.
4 Briefcase left in full view in the back window of the car.
5 Several days' supply of milk bottles a sign that the owner is away.
6 Newspapers in the letterbox – also a sign that the owner is away.
7 Curtains and blinds drawn in the daytime – another sign of absence.
8 Tools left in an open garage – these could help the burglar to enter.
9 Ladder left where it will make things easy for the thief
10 The note in the letter box of No. 35 tells the world that the house is empty.

Recap by asking students to translate the points into pieces of advice. For example: When you go away on holiday, you should make sure you close all the windows, cancel the newspapers, etc.

Note: Don't ask the students to put these instructions in writing at this stage, as they form part of the task in the Focus on writing section of this unit.

▶Text 1 · Seven banks a day are robbed in LA (p. 47)

2 *a* It has far more (bank robberies) than any other American city.
  b It was the last day that Los Angeles didn't have a bank robbery.
  c The city has a large number of banks. They provide a lot of opportunities for robbers by staying open late in the evening and at weekends. They also tend to have a relaxed atmosphere.

3 Vocabulary

a fond	*i* surveillance
b haul	*j* makes a getaway
c heads	*k* freeway
d league	*l* heads
e appreciative	*m* squad
f genteel	*n* bandit
g teller	*o* doffs
h pockets	

4 True/false

- *a* False. (The figure refers to business days and is, in any case, only an average.)
- *b* False. ('None of the machine-gun violence of the old movies'.)
- *c* True. ('Tellers have orders to hand over the money immediately'.)
- *d* False. ('"The banks believe, quite rightly, ..." says one FBI man'.)
- *e* False. ('a smile in the direction of the cameras')
- *f* False. (It was only the last single day without a robbery.)
- *g* True. ('The robber passes a stick-up note to a teller'.)
- *h* True. ('They are also very informal'.)

5 *a* He has succeeded in committing so many robberies that he may have created a record. He also makes a habit of smiling at the cameras.
  b To buy drugs.
  c They drive away (on to nearby freeways).

6 *a* Because he has committed so many robberies and also, perhaps, because he makes the FBI look foolish.
  b Perhaps 'This is a bank raid. Don't press the alarm or call for help. Give me $ ...'

Vocabulary included in the Vocabulary review: to head (13, 40), an *awful lot* (16), *do* business (20), to hand over (31), *in* the direction of (47).

▶Focus on grammar 1 · Modal verbs 2: obligation (p. 48)

Passage

you *have to* pay; you *should* allow; you *don't* usually *have to* pay; You *must* complete; you *needn't* send

Exercise 1

a must	*e* must
b had to	*f* have to
c I've had to	
d has to	

Exercise 2

a needn't/don't have to	*d* mustn't; needn't/don't have to
b mustn't	*e* mustn't
c needn't/don't have to	

Exercise 3

- *a* didn't need to go
- *b* didn't need to buy *or* didn't have to buy
- *c* needn't have written
- *d* didn't need to have *or* didn't have to have
- *e* needn't have damaged

Exercise 4

- *a* You *mustn't* smoke in here.
- *b* You ('ll) *have to* get a visa before you travel.
- *c* I *needn't have done* all this cooking!
- *d* You *must* go to bed now, children.
- *e* You *needn't/dont have to* reserve a table.

▶Focus on writing 1 · Speech (p. 49)

Review the main features of this kind of writing with the class, such as the importance of identifying
– **who** you are
– who **your audience** is
– **where** you are
– **what** you're talking about
and of designing the speech to fit these features. Stress the importance of typical features of spoken English such as contractions and 'filler' phrases.

Ask students to work together to make notes for the **middle paragraphs**. Check these with the class.

Set the writing task either in class or for homework.

As with the previous writing exercise of this type, you may like to give one or two students the opportunity to deliver their speeches to the class at a later stage.

► **Focus on listening 1 · Crime report** (p. 50)

Check that students understand the instructions before playing the tape.

The following numbers should be ticked: 3, 5, 7, 8, 10, 12. The following numbers should have a cross: 2, 6, 8. (Marks should be deducted for any numbers wrongly marked.)

When you are checking the answers make sure that students can say **why** the other numbers should not have ticks or crosses, since this is just as important to the exercise as marking the correct numbers.

Useful vocabulary: with the exception of; missing, break into (see Study Box 3), a handful of, a bargain price, get away (see Study Box 2), to trace, file, spanner, hammer, to jog a person's memory, a saloon car.

► **Text 2 · You're already well equipped to prevent crime** (p. 50)

Multiple-choice

1 *d*
2 *b* (Many of us go around with the alarm switched off. We don't see … We overlook … We don't notice …)
3 *c* (the stranger loitering … the kids trying the car doors … the sounds from the flat upstairs)
4 *c* (… you know more … than the police ever could)
5 *b* (It's early days yet, but results so far are very encouraging.)

Note: Not *a*: 'Wherever' is not the same as 'many of the areas'.

Vocabulary included in the Vocabulary review: keep a look-out.

Describing clothes

A	shorts	G	raincoat
B	skirt	H	collar
C	trousers (man) or	I	blouse
	slacks (woman)	J	overalls
D	sleeve	K	cap
E	jacket	L	belt
F	T shirt		

Note: These are the main clothing items listed in the *Cambridge English Lexicon*, but you (or the students) may want to expand the list.

For extra practice, ask students to describe each other using the tenses in the examples.

► **Communication activity · Witness** (p. 52)

Notes

This activity serves, among other things, to alert students to gaps in their knowledge of language for describing people. It creates a need for the relevant language and makes students especially receptive to subsequent teaching. For this reason, it is **not** a good idea to pre-teach special vocabulary or refer students to the Functions Bank beforehand.

The activity also provides useful practice for Part I of Paper 5 in the exam (the Interview).

Procedure

First explain how the activity will work orally. Then ask students to read the introduction and check that they understand exactly what to do.

Students usually need little if any help with the activity, but it is useful to monitor their progress and to note down any language gaps they have.

Make sure each pair has looked at the picture together before they change roles. Monitor the class as before.

At the end, discuss the results briefly and deal with any vocabulary problems the students had.

Who makes the best witness?

Again check that students understand the introduction before they start the pair work. It is also a good idea to elicit one or two more examples like the one given before pairwork begins.

Refer students to the Functions Bank on page 214. Depending on your students' needs, you may want to deal with this language in greater depth.

Students could be asked to produce written comparisons for class or homework.

The main difference between the two groups was that the police remembered the two people's appearance very accurately but were less accurate in recalling what actually happened. In fact, they remembered **more** than what actually happened, with details that weren't there. The situation with the public was almost exactly the reverse.

These findings are the result of a real experiment!

► **Focus on listening 2 · Bad start to a honeymoon** (p. 53)

Pre-check the word 'honeymoon'.

1 (To) the airport.
2 tickets

tickets	✓	credit card	✓
passports	✓	cash	
travellers' cheques		cheque book	✓
flight bag	✓	driving licence	
suitcases	✓	marriage licence	

3 Some friends.
4 Under a blanket.
5 Because his father is a senior policeman.
6 No.
7 A winter coat.
8 She works in a bank.
9 *c* 'They've managed to fix us up with another holiday, in Rhodes …'
10 *a* '… things can only get better after this!', '… it's marvellous to be married.'

► **Text 3 · Granny, 70, holds up a bank!** (p. 54)

1 In court, she denied that she had attacked a customer (She admitted … assaulting …)
4 She pretended that she had a gun.
7 She was arrested.
   She bought a ticket on the bus to Kensington. (She used her pensioner's pass.)
6 She agreed to accept £50,000.
1 Mrs Barlow got into debt.
3 She took a customer as a hostage.
9 A court found her guilty.
5 She asked for all the money in the bank.
8 She asked to make a telephone call.
2 She saw a programme about robberies on television.
   She told the judge that she was sorry. (She apologised to the bank staff.)

2 **Example answers**

a She had serious money problems and she got the idea of robbing a bank from a television programme.
b She made them think she had a gun.
c Her hostage managed to overcome the bank robber. The bank manager had left the office, so he probably called the police while this was happening.
d She was given a suspended sentence. This means that she was found guilty but the judge didn't actually send her to prison to serve her sentence. So long as she behaved well and didn't break the law again, she could go free.
e She seems to find it hard to believe that she actually did it. She certainly thinks it was very stupid of her.

f This robber was a respectable elderly lady. She travelled by bus, not by car. She only pretended to have a gun. She apologised to bank staff afterwards. She *asked* for the money rather than using a stick-up note. She took a hostage. (And so on.)

Vocabulary included in the Vocabulary review: hostage (3), turn out to be (7), to bundle (24), settle for (32), a (prison) sentence/to sentence (49), admit + ing (51).

▶ Focus on grammar 2 · Participles (p. 55)

2 *a inviting* place
  b working
  c built-in burglar alarm
  d Bespectacled widow
  e stolen chequebook

Exercise 1

a tiring
b ground
c long-lasting
d worn
e well-known
f frightening
g helping
h broken
i brightly-lit
j warning

Exercise 2 (Example answers)

a Crossing
b Having worked
c Looking out of
d Waiting
e Not knowing
f Having spent
g Seeing
h Having tried

Exercise 3

a (While) *unloading* the car after the holiday, we realised ...
b She rushed to answer the phone, *knowing* that it might be ...
c *Having taken* my name and address, the sergeant asked me ...
d *Not finding* anyone at home, she pushed a note ...
e *Having eaten* a three-course meal already, I had to refuse ...
f *Tearing* open the letter, he found ...
g *Thinking* that I had stolen the bag, the shop assistant called ...
h *Not being* used to the climate, I found it ...

▶ Focus on writing 2 · Description (p. 57)

Preparation

Check that students understand **exactly** what to do. Marks are often lost in the examination when students fail to read the instructions for a piece of writing carefully enough.

It is useful to have a class planning session when students can discuss their appearance and clothes with each other and can check on any vocabulary they might need.

▶ Vocabulary review (p. 58)

1 *c* (1.47/48)
2 *b* (1.20)
3 *b* (1.16)
4 *d* (1.13)
5 *d* (1.31)
6 *d* (3.24)
7 *b* (3.3)
8 *d* (Study Box 1)
9 *a* (3.32)
10 *c* (3.49)
11 *a* (3.51)
12 *b* (3.7)
13 *a* (2)
14 *c* (Describing clothes)
15 *c* (Study Box 2)

UNIT **5A** Waste not, want not

▶ Lead-in (p. 59)

1 *a* bottle (perfume, vinegar)
  b tube (toothpaste, glue)
  c box (chocolate, matches)
  d bag (sugar, potatoes)
  e carton (milk, orange-juice)
  f jar (instant coffee, honey)
  g packet (tea, envelopes)
  h tin (soup, peaches)

Note: Several of the items above can, of course, be bought in more than one type of container, for example, milk (bottle, carton), glue (tube, jar).

2 **What is packaging for? (Example answers)**

To protect the contents.
To give instructions for use.
To hold a definite amount.
To tell you what the contents are.
To make you want to buy the product.

The purpose of the task is not to find a number of 'right' answers but to discuss various issues concerned with packaging. For example:
How much packaging is unnecessary?
How much information on packaging is useful?
How much are we influenced by packaging in deciding what to buy?
What are the negative effects of packaging?

Discuss the results of the pairwork briefly before going on to Text 1.

▶ Text 1 · One-Trip Living (p. 59)

1 **Pre-questions**

a It refers to the large number of products which are designed to be used only once and then thrown away.
b They create an enormous amount of waste and cost the customer more.
c The manufacturers of containers.

2 *a* rural
  b permanent
  c shipped
  d trend
  e the rising tide
  f reimburse
  g promoting
  h bonfire
  i purchased
  j disposable

3 *a* Because methods of food production have changed and it's not possible to collect many foods from one place any more. There are a great many more types of food available than there used to be, and pre-cooked meals have become very popular.
b When they bought a soft drink, they paid a deposit for the bottle and they later got their deposit back when they returned the bottle.
c Yes, because sales of the new soft drinks bottles increased.
d The glass manufacturers arranged to pay back most of the cost of the new bottles to the bottling companies.
e There's no need to clean them after use.
f The writer seems to recognise that disposable products are more convenient but s/he also mentions the extra cost involved in producing them and the increased amount of rubbish that they create. In addition, the question at the end suggests that the writer is worried about the way that the trend is spreading.

4 *a* For example, bowls, jars, buckets, etc.
  b For example, ball-point pens, lighters, razors, paper handkerchiefs, etc.

Vocabulary included in the Vocabulary review: unless (5), to last (6), replace (with) (26).

▶ Focus on grammar 1 · Conditional 1 (p. 61)

1 You may prefer to elicit suitable examples and focus on the **form** on the board, rather than have students reading through this section in the book.

2 *a* freezes
  b drop it in water
  c boils
  d lights/ignites
  e For example, don't water them
  f For example, eat too much

3
1 *e*	3 *f*	5 *i*	7 *j*	9 *g*
2 *h*	4 *a*	6 *c*	8 *d*	10 *b*

Conditional 1

1 Again, you may prefer to present this section on the board rather than by asking students to read through the notes in the book.

2 *a* I'*ll give* you a ring if I *need* any advice.
  b He *can only come* if the meeting *takes* place on a Friday.
  c If you *don't pass* the examination, *will you take* it again?
  d She'*ll just have to* take a taxi if she *misses* the train.
  e If you *go* to see him now, he'*ll be working.*
  f We'*ll lose* our way if we *don't keep* to the main road.
  g If the weather *is* sunny, we'*ll have brought* our umbrellas for nothing.
  h If you *don't speak* clearly, he *won't be able to* understand.

3 Example answers
  a If you find 'Tibbles', you'll receive a reward of £25.
  b If you park there, you'll have to pay a fine of £50.
  c If you enter the photography competition, you'll have a chance of winning £1,000.
  d If you haven't got a visitor's pass, you won't be able to go in.
  e If you have two garments cleaned in this shop, you'll only have to pay for one of them.
  f If you drink the contents of that bottle, you'll die.

4 *a* unless
  b Suppose
  c as long as/provided (that)
  d For example, (that) the weather is good.
  e For example, you lose your ticket.
  f For example, they know where I am.
  g For example, you pay me back in a month.

▶ Focus on listening 1 · The sweet, short life of products (p. 62)

A possible lead-in is to ask students to discuss (in pairs) how long they have had their cameras, bicycles, etc. Ask them to suggest what is the life span of these products and write their answers on the board.

Give students time to read the instructions and the questions, and check that they understand what to do and that there are no vocabulary problems.

1 A light bulb.
2 A new style, colour or extra improvements.
3 (The) fashion and car (industries).
4 The kitchen.

The Useful Life of Products (in years)

Products	Useful life of product (manufacturer's estimate)	Actual time in use in the USA	Actual time used in underdeveloped countries
a Washing machines and irons	5	5	25
b Cars	11	2.2	40+
c bicycles	25	2	75
d Construction equipment	14	8	100+
e ships	30	15	80+
f Photographic equipment	35	1.1	50

▶ Communication activity 1 · Pollution (p. 63)

Note: This activity provides practice in describing a picture for Paper 5 in the examination (the interview).

The students have their books closed. Explain the activity and make sure that students understand **what** they have to do and **how** they're going to do it.

Tell students who to work with and, if possible, rearrange seating so that students are facing each other. If this is not possible, ask them to mask their books so that their partner cannot see their picture.

Assign roles A and B in each pair and tell students which pages to turn to.

The students open their books and begin. Monitor the activity, making sure that students are describing their pictures in enough detail and that they are asking each other questions. Make sure too, that one student in each pair is writing down a list of the differences they find.

Give help if necessary by supplying unknown vocabulary or by indicating an area of the picture that could be examined more closely.

If a pair finds five differences fairly quickly, they may prefer to go on and find as many more as they can **without** looking at the pictures. If they have taken more time to find five, remind them that they can now find the rest by comparing the two pictures.

Differences in B's picture (from left to right)
1 Man is smoking a cigar, not a cigarette.
2 Woman is spraying flowers with left hand.
3 There are only 4 rubbish bags, not 5.
4 Woman shopper has a shoulder bag, not a shopping bag.
5 Stripes on teenager's shirt are different.
6 No picture of a burger above the shop sign.
7 Traffic sign is different.
8 Car registration number is different.

Checking

Ask students to describe each difference accurately and establish relevant vocabulary from the list above.

Check other useful vocabulary illustrated in the picture, for example window box, aerosol can, dustbin, pavement, kerb, radio-cassette player, exhaust fumes.

Ask students what examples of pollution they can see in the picture, for example noise pollution (music and cars), air pollution (factory smoke, exhaust fumes and aerosol spray), litter.

Vocabulary included in the Vocabulary review: wear out, *persuade* someone *to do* something.

Other useful vocabulary: out of date, to cash in, scarce, to break down, to patch, to replace … *with*, vital, to shrink.

▶ Text 2 · Recycling (p. 64)

1 *c* (Section B)
2 *d* (Section H – 'almost impossible to separate for recycling')
3 *d* (Section I – their deposit is returned, making the drinks cheaper)
4 *b* (Section K – they are ground and remelted)
5 *a* (Section G – imported paper can be cheaper when the pound is strong)
6 *c* (Section J – Alcan will send you the address of your nearest collection centre)

Vocabulary
7 *a*
8 *c*
9 *c*
10 *b*

▶Text 3 (p. 66)

True/false

a True **and** false. (It's one aim but not the only one.)
b False. (It's one danger, but there are many others.)
c True. ('About half the world's animal and plant species could be extinct.')
d False. (Forests the size of Wales, not in Wales.)
e False. ('New jobs would be created . . .')
f True.
g True **and** false. (Bicycles are recommended for short journeys.)
h True. ('Cycleways should be built . . .')

Vocabulary included in the Vocabulary review: be/become aware of (3), to waste (6), resources (7), cut down (17), spend . . . *on* (28).

▶Focus on grammar 2 · Conditional 2 (p. 66)

As in the previous grammar section, you may prefer to present the example(s) and form on the board.

Exercise 1

a Your uncle would really appreciate it if you *went* to see him.
b If she *made* more effort to help herself, *I'd have* more sympathy with her.
c Chris *wouldn't take* a day off work unless he *was/were* really ill.
d If you *knew* her as well as I do, you *wouldn't rely* on her at all!
e We'd *have to* reduce the price if we *wanted* to sell our house quickly.
f If electric cars *didn't have* such large batteries, they*'d be* faster to drive.
g If you *called* the Fire Brigade, how long *would it take* them to arrive?
h I *wouldn't carry* your wallet around in your pocket if I *were* you.

Exercise 2

First ask students to say what's wrong about Martin's appearance.

long hair	scruffy shoes
unshaven	shoe lace undone
sunglasses	striped socks
crooked tie	bulging pockets

Suggested answers

If he	straightened his tie shaved/had a shave took off his sunglasses changed his socks/put on plain socks did up his shoe lace emptied his pockets cleaned his shoes/wore smarter shoes	, he'd . . .

▶Focus on writing · Discussion (p. 67)

Work through the preparation phase, stage by stage, allowing the students plenty of oral practice. Monitor the work of groups and pairs.

1 At the end of stage 1, draw up a list of students' suggestions on the board so that there is a wide range of types of pollution for students to refer to.
2 Again, check students' ideas about **who is responsible** before they practise explaining causes.
3 Again, collate students' ideas on the effects of pollution, possible solutions and problems on the board before they practise orally, using language from the tables.

▶Communication activity 2 · Follow the country code (p. 68)

Ask students to suggest what the term Country Code means. Unless they can do this at once, remind them of the similar expression, Highway Code, and give one or two examples from it, such as: Look in your mirror before you overtake to make sure it's

safe to do so. (You could elicit one or two more.) Ask what a *code* is (a list of rules).

Students can either perform the task individually and compare their answers afterwards, or work together from the start.

When checking the answers, ask students to explain their choices by describing what they can see in the pictures.

Keep your dogs under control.	3	**K**eep to public paths across farmland.	4
Help to keep all water clean.	8	**G**uard against all risk of fire.	1
Take your litter home.	7	**T**ake special care on country roads.	10
Fasten all gates.	2	**P**rotect wildlife, plants and trees.	9
Leave livestock, crops and machinery alone.	6	**U**se gates and stiles to cross fences, hedges and walls.	5

Example sentences

a If you left litter lying about, it would spoil the view for other people.
b If you didn't fasten gates behind you, cattle might escape.
c If you didn't keep to public paths across farmland, you might damage crops.
d If you drove carelessly on country roads, you might injure an animal.
e If you didn't use gates and stiles, you might damage fences, hedges or walls.

Vocabulary included in the Vocabulary review: *under* control, leave . . . *alone*, keep to.

▶Focus on listening 2 (p. 69)

Part one

1 c
2 a LD
  b S
  c PD
  d PC (the most densely populated
  e PD (the most heavily used)
  f N (Hadrian's Wall)
  g S
  h N

Part two

		A 1	**B** 2
C 3	**D** 4	**E** X	**F** 6
G 5	**H** X	**I** X	**J** 7

Note: Part two contains a number of words and phrases describing shapes, and it would be a good time to revise and practise these. There is a full list on pages 212–213 of the Functions Bank.

▶Focus on grammar 3 · Modal verbs 2: permission (p. 70)

1 a a public footpath
  b take a pram or pushchair . . . take a dog which is not on a lead.
  c go on horseback
  d could

Practice

Note: You may also like to refer students to the Functions Bank, page 210, for other ways of asking for, and giving permission.

Example answers

a Can I borrow your ruler for a minute?
  – No, (I'm sorry you can't,) because I'm using it.
b May I come in?
  – Yes, of course.
c Excuse me, I wonder if I could use your telephone? My car's broken down.
  – Yes, of course. Come in.
d Excuse me. Could I (possibly) look at your map for a moment?
  – Yes, do.
e Can I (Do you mind if I) go across your field?
  – No, you most certainly can't! (Yes, I certainly do!)
f Could I drive your new car?
  – No, you can't!

 g Could I possibly interrupt for a second?
  – Yes, of course.
 h I wonder if I could possibly borrow £100 – just for two days?
  – No, I'm awfully sorry, but I'm rather hard up at the moment.

▶ Vocabulary review (p. 72)

1 *b* (Communication activity 2) **9** *b* (3)
2 *d* (Communication activity 2) **10** *d* (3)
3 *a* (Communication activity 2) **11** *c* (1.6)
4 *c* (Listening 1) **12** *b* (Grammar 3)
5 *b* (Listening 1) **13** *a* (3)
6 *d* (Lead-in 2) **14** *c* (3)
7 *c* (1.6) **15** *d* (1.26)
8 *a* (3)

UNIT **6A** The shape of things to come

▶ Lead-in (p. 73)

1 Encourage students not to spend too long or read too thoroughly, but simply to find answers to the five questions as quickly as possible. Check the questions beforehand if necessary.
 a No. The robot is for 'home entertainment'.
 b In the home.
 c A battery.
 d No information.
 e The department stores and other shops listed.

2 *a* Yes ('voice ... transmission', 'He will ... talk to your friends').
 b No.
 c Yes ('he will fetch and carry drinks').
 d Yes ('digital display and alarm system').
 e Yes ('micro-computer for movement control').
 f No.
 g Yes ('play your favourite cassettes').
 h Yes ('7 day memory').
 i No.
 j Yes ('alarm system', 'wake the kids up').
 k No.
 l No.

Optional writing task

Imagine that your OMNIBOT has been stolen. Write a statement for the police, explaining the circumstances in which it was stolen and including an exact description of the robot. (about 200 words)

Note: Students might find it helpful to refer to the Functions Bank for the language of describing shape and location (page 212).

Vocabulary included in the Vocabulary review: obey, fetch, deliver, *get* to know, well/best-behaved.

▶ Focus on grammar 1 · Talking about the future (p. 74)

Exercise 1
 a are you going to wear/are your wearing
 b I'm having/going to have
 c I'm not taking
 d We are having/going to have
 e Are you doing/going to do
 f aren't you going
 g is playing
 h are you going to do

Exercise 2 (Example answers)
 a 's going to be a storm.
 b is going to break
 c isn't going to bite me.
 d 's going to be an accident.
 e 're going to run out of
 f 'm going to sneeze.
 g is going to be a draw.
 h isn't going to be a strike.

Exercise 3 (Example answers)
 a How *do we get to* Dover?
 b Which French port *do we travel to?*
 c What time *do we arrive in* Paris?
 d What *happens on* the first evening?
 e What *do we do on* Monday?
 f Where *do we go on* Tuesday?
 g What *do we see in* the afternoon?
 h When *do we leave for* Epernay?
 i What else *do we do* there?
 j What time *do we arrive back in* London?
 k Where *do we stop* during the trip?
 l Are there any extras that *we have to pay for?*

Note: If your students have made a lot of mistakes with prepositions in Exercise 3, it would be a good time to revise prepositions of time and place, for example:

at 6 o'clock, night, etc.
on Monday, Monday evening, etc.
in the afternoon, etc.
live *in*
arrive *in* (large city)
arrive *at* (smaller place)
travel *to*

▶ Text 1 · The robot wine waiter that lost its head (p. 75)

(Pre-questions)

1 Example answer

There's a man who seems to be pushing a strange machine. It must be a robot which has been designed to look like a waiter. The robot has got a round head with eyes, nose and a mouth painted on. It's got two arms and seems to be carrying a sort of tray. There are various controls on its chest The base of the robot is triangular in shape. He's wearing a hat and a bow tie.

Check to see if students know the idiomatic meaning of 'to lose one's head' (to behave wildly) as well as the literal one.

1 True/false

a False. (It spilled a glass of wine on its first test run.)
b True. (It became uncontrollable.)
c False. (An engineer demonstrated the robot.)
d True. (It just needed practice, and in time you can perfect it.)
e False. (He said that if the batteries were undercharged, the results would be catastrophic.)
f True. (batteries)
g True. ('incapable of speech or movement').
h False. ('After the case was settled, …')

2 Vocabulary matching

a ran amok
b erratic
c failed
d perfect
e conjuring trick

f catastrophic
g jerky
h a sorry state
i trolley
j detached from

Discussion points

These points can be discussed in pairs, small groups, or by the class as a whole.

Examples of automatic machines replacing people are: coffee machines, self-service petrol pumps, bank cash dispensers.

Vocabulary included in the Vocabulary review: was *supposed* to (1), knock over (2).

▶ Focus on listening 1 · Word processor mishaps (p. 77)

1 Word processing

it	would
takes	but
use	For
on	be
Then/Next/Later	with
of	for

a You can correct mistakes and make changes without having to re-type your work. You can also store your work on a disk for future use.

b You use a keyboard like a typewriter but the words appear on a *screen* rather than on paper. You also need a separate *printer* to print out the text, and *disks*.

2

	A	B	C	D
a Profession	Cookery Writer	Journalist	Novelist	TV Reporter
b Make of Machine	✗	Astra	Rocket 22	✗
c What was lost	50 Recipes	an article	2 Chapters	Script for a documentary

d

	A	B	C	D
A fault of the machine			✓	
The speaker's mistake	✓			
Someone else's mistake		✓		
Another reason (say what it was)				a burglary

e A (Cookery writer).

Vocabulary included in the Vocabulary review: *as far as* I'm concerned, cut off (see also Study Box 2).

▶ Focus on writing 1 · Instructions (p. 77)

Ask students to work in pairs and discuss the steps which the pictures show.

Check results and practice instructions for the first three pictures orally. Draw students' attention to the sequence markers and vocabulary under *Useful language*. If your students need more help, go through all the instructions orally first.

Example answer

First, lift the systems box carefully out of the carton and place it on a flat surface, removing the polystyrene packaging from the sides. Next, remove the polythene wrapping from the monitor and place the monitor in the groove on top of the systems box. Check that the power is switched off before connecting the monitor to the systems box by plugging in the power flex. After that, unwrap the keyboard and place it in front of the systems box. Finally, adjust the position of the monitor so that it is convenient for you to work at.

▶ Focus on grammar 2 · Sudden decisions, offers, suggestions, threats (p. 78)

Exercise (Example answers)

a Shall I open the window? (Offer)
b I'll look it up in the dictionary. (Sudden decision)
c I'll take it away from you. (Threat)
d Shall I give it some water? (Offer/Suggestion)
e I'll pay for it to be cleaned. (Promise)
f Shall I see who it is? (Offer)
g I'll clear it up. (Promise)
h Shall I phone the Fire Brigade? (Suggestion)
i I'll report you to the Police! (Threat)
j Shall I book a hotel for you? (Offer)

▶ Text 2 · The £100 car telephone (p. 79)

Multiple-choice

1 *d*
2 *b* (volume controls)
3 *d* (electronic lock)
4 *b* (call timer, charge time stored)
5 *d* (3-way conversations)
6 *c* (both hands on the steering wheel)

Vocabulary included in the Vocabulary review: a (good) deal, engaged, volume *controls*, no *need* to.

▶ Communication activity 1 · Role play (p. 80)

Note: This activity involves an information gap and, for this reason, it's best if the procedure is explained thoroughly before students start reading the instructions in the book.

Preparation

Students have their books closed. Explain to them that they are going to work in pairs, one as salesman/woman for an office equipment company, one as the boss of the company. Check 'office equipment' by asking what the company might sell (for example, desks, filing cabinets, typewriters, etc.).

Tell students that their instructions are on different pages of the book and that they should read them carefully before beginning the role play. They should not show their instructions to their partner!

Optional extra stage: You may like to make use of the Functions Bank for preliminary language practice. The following sections are relevant, but remind students of the need for a certain degree of formality between boss and employee: Agreeing/Disagreeing (pages 208–209); Making and Responding to Suggestions (page 210); Expressing Need and Use (page 211).

Decide which students should work in pairs and allot roles A and B. Tell A students to turn to page 80, B students to page 86. Students open their books. Check with individual pairs that they have understood their instructions before they begin.

An alternative approach is to ask all students with A and B roles to form two groups and discuss any problems before they begin. Again, check with each group to answer any questions before pairwork begins.

Role play

Monitor the role play unobtrusively and make a note of any language problems which arise. It is best not to interrupt or interfere unless absolutely necessary.

Feedback

Ask students to comment on the conversation they have had and the results. Deal with any language problems you have noted.

▶ Focus on listening 2 · The year 2000 (p. 81)

Give students time to read the instructions and questions, and check that these are understood before playing the tape.

1

	First group	Second group
space travel	✓	
robots	✓	
computers	✓	✓
nuclear weapons	✓	✓
overpopulation	✓	✓

	First group	Second group
test tube babies		
unemployment	✓	
future places for people to live	✓	✓
future forms of energy		
future forms of communication		✓

2 *b* **3** *c* **4** *c* **5** *d*

Vocabulary included in the Vocabulary review: go wrong *with*.

▶ Focus on grammar 3 · Talking about the future 2 (p. 81)

Exercise 3 (Example answers)

 a It's no use going then because the sale will have finished.
 b It's no good going to the bank then because it will have closed.
 c It's no good leaving at midnight because the last train will have left.
 d There's no point in getting there at midday because my train won't have arrived yet.
 e There's no point in phoning me on the 15th because I won't have taken the exam by then.

Exercise 4

 a I'll have heard the results
 b it will probably cause some damage

 c I'll be swimming
 d I'll give you a hand
 e we'll have been married
 f what do you think will happen
 g they'll just be getting up/they'll just have got up
 h What are you going to do/will you do
 i Will the builders have finished
 j I doubt if you will get home

▶ Communication activity 2 · Describe and draw (p. 84)

Preparation

Read through the introduction and instructions with the students and make sure they are understood.

If necessary, revise basic vocabulary for describing buildings – roof, chimney, windows, floors etc.

You may prefer to elicit the key language for expressing location and describing shape and put this on the board, rather than refer students to the Functions Bank.

Make sure students are facing each other and cannot see each other's books. Point out that basic shapes are required, not artistic masterpieces!

Pairwork

Monitor the activity carefully and be prepared to help students who have difficulties. Encourage them to ask and answer questions. Note any particular language problems which arise.

Feedback

At the end of each drawing phase, ask students to compare their pictures with the original and discuss any differences. Ask if there was any vocabulary which they felt they needed.

▶ Focus on writing 2 · Description/discussion (p. 84)

Preparation

It's useful to have a planning stage during which students can make suggestions and pool their ideas. A good way of doing this is to arrange students in small groups of 3–5 to discuss possible developments. They should base their discussion on the topics listed for the middle paragraphs. Tell them to make notes and be prepared to report back to the rest of the class afterwards.

During the discussion, monitor, make suggestions if necessary and encourage students to use appropriate language for expressing opinions and making predictions about the future. For example:
  I think/I don't think there'll be …
  I think telephones will probably have screens …
  People may retire at 35.

After this groupwork, ask students to report back. Write up interesting ideas and useful vocabulary on the board.

▶ Vocabulary review (p. 85)

1 *d* (Lead-in)
2 *c* (2. Carphone 6000)
3 *a* (Lead-in)
4 *a* (Lead-in)
5 *c* (Grammar 3)
6 *b* (Lead-in)
7 *b* (Listening 1)
8 *c* (Listening 1)
9 *d* (Lead-in)
10 *b* (Listening 2)
11 *c* (1.11)
12 *d* (2. Carphone 2000)
13 *b* (1.1)
14 *a* (2. Carphone 4000)
15 *d* (2 Introduction)

UNIT 1B Going the hard way

▶Lead-in (p. 87)

1 The four pictures and their accompanying questions provide practice for the first part of Paper 5 in the exam, the Interview.

For questions *a* and *b*, encourage students to make full use of the information in the pictures and to give detailed rather than general answers, as far as possible. Point out that it isn't necessary to know the exact word to describe something, as long as you can make the meaning clear.

Go through the answers to questions *a* and *b* for picture A, showing how much information can be used and helping with vocabulary as necessary. Then ask students in pairs or small groups of 3 or 4 to work together to answer the same questions for pictures B to D.

Example answer, picture A

The picture shows a man on skis in a snowy region. It could be the Arctic or the Antarctic. He's standing near a flag and throwing his arms up into the air. Behind him there's something which looks like a sledge with his equipment on it, probably. There doesn't seem to be anyone with him, apart from the photographer, that is!

He's completely covered up to protect himself from the cold. He's got a thick jacket and trousers on. His head is covered so that you can't even see his face. He's wearing gloves and boots.

For questions *c–g*, encourage students to use the language of speculation rather than only the terms 'probably' or 'maybe':

it he they	might could may	be … have …	he	might could may	have (done)
he it	seems + adjective		he it	seems to	be have
he it	looks like + noun		he it	looks as if + clause	

Revise the language of speculation, using questions *c* and *d* as examples. Then ask the same pairs/groups as before to work out answers for questions *e*, *f* and *g*.

Example answer, picture A (question *c*)

The flag means that he must be British. He could have reached some special place for the first time. It can't be the top of a mountain because he wouldn't have a sledge with him then. It might be somewhere like the North Pole.

Example answer, picture A (question *d*)

He seems to be shouting out in joy because he has achieved something which is very difficult to do. He might be saying 'I've done it! I've reached the North Pole.'

2 The completed table is as follows. (*Note*: The last line cannot be completed until students have read through the extracts in task 5.)

	Picture A	Picture B	Picture C	Picture D
1 Method of travel	skis	motorbike	bicycle	boat
2 Destination	North Pole	Africa	Australia	China
3 Stores list	c	a	d	b
4 Extract	D	B	A	C

3 **Example answers**

   a 5 gallon jerrycan of petrol
   b several novels, metal suitcase
   c gloves, radio, satellite relay kit, 200 kilos of food, rifle
   d cycle spares

5 See the table above.

6 *a* Perhaps because the village people had never seen

Westerners before, so they were interested to meet and welcome them.
   b Learning how to handle the bikes in different conditions.
   c Examples: inner tubes (for tyres), chains, etc.
   d They spread (distributed) the load they were carrying so that it was well balanced.
   e Because he didn't want to travel on the well-known routes from England or Holland, and there was a convenient boat from Athens which he could take on his way to the Suez Canal.
   f A steamer – a ship which is driven by steam power.
   g Difficult, 'a formidable major *hurdle*'.
   h Intense cold, tiredness, poor visibility, loss of radio contact with people who could help him, the fact that his compass isn't working.
   i He wanted to be the first person to go there alone on foot.

Vocabulary included in Exam practice A: a load/to load (extract *b*), spare (extract *b*).

▶Text 1 · Freezing (p. 89)

Optional pre-questions

  1 What was the cause of the problem?
  2 What happened to Rick?
  3 What happened to save him?

Suggested answers

  1 The freezing cold (temperatures).
  2 He collapsed from the cold.
  3 An Algerian man took him to a camp in the mountains where he was able to warm up by a fire, drink coffee and eat biscuits.

2 **True/false**

   a False. (they had a tent)
   b True. ('colder and colder until … impossible to sleep')
   c True. (wearing every article of clothing we had with us')
   d True and false. (They felt warmer 'but only for a few minutes')
   e False. (he 'came to a halt' before falling (through coldness))
   f False. ('he 'worked to bring his companion round')
   g False. ('he was clearly in danger')
   h True. ('before he had a chance to say anything')
   i False. ('David was aware of somebody approaching')
   j True. (David was 'convinced that Rick would have died if it hadn't been for that man')

Vocabulary included in Exam practice A: wrap up (16), bring a person round (43/44) (see also Study Box 3), response (45), take control of (66/67), *make* an effort (77).

▶Focus on listening 1 · Overland to Australia (p. 90)

Allow students time to read through the eight questions and to ask anything they might want to. Point out that question 2 refers to countries passed through *more than once*.

  1 *d*
  2 Turkey, Syria, Jordan
  3 Iran, India, Australia
  4 *c*
  5 visas, clothes, injections
  6 all accommodation, food, transport
  7 *c*
  8 *d*

▶Text 2 · Trisha Greenhalgh (p. 91)

Pre-questions

   a They had to cross a narrow bridge over a pond.
   b Mat rode straight over but Trisha stopped because she was afraid that she might fall in.
   c Mat left Trisha to overcome her fear alone and, in the end, she did.

Note: You may prefer to do the vocabulary matching exercise next if your students need more help.

Multiple-choice

  1 *b* ('nothing to stop us falling … if we overbalanced')

2 *d* ('If I slip, I'll be in there ...')
3 *a* ('There's nothing to it.')
4 *b* ('he would give me at least an hour before coming to help.')
5 *c* ('To remain stationary ... was suicide')

Vocabulary matching

a	blazing	*f*	bog
b	stifling	*g*	yelled
c	rickety	*h*	sickly
d	stagnant	*i*	stationary
e	sleepers	*j*	obstacles

Vocabulary included in Exam practice A: steam/to steam (8), What's *up*? (14), to slip (16), nothing *to* it (18), sweat/to sweat (28).

▶ Focus on grammar 1 · The gerund (p. 92)

Exercise 1

a	by	*d*	of
b	before	*e*	without
c	after		

Exercise 2

a	*of* earning/making	*e*	*on* paying (for)
b	*without* asking/getting	*f*	*with* working
c	*for* cutting	*g*	*from* joining/working in, etc.
d	*at* remembering	*h*	*in* getting/finding, etc.

Exercise 3 (Example answers)

a paying it
b riding horses
c taking some family photos, etc.
d looking after kids/youngsters, etc.

(Gerunds after verbs)
Exercise 1

a	3	*e*	2
b	5	*f*	8
c	4	*g*	1
d	7	*h*	6

Exercise 2 (Example answers)

a going to the cinema so often
b ironing
c stroking them
d falling off from time to time
e whistling
f working underground all day
g reading it
h stealing the money
i looking it up in the directory
j making it sound an attractive place to visit

▶ Communication activity · Quiz (p. 93)

It might be helpful to pre-teach *redundancy*, *redundancy pay* and *pay rise* to help students understand question 12.

Read through the introduction with the class and make sure they understand why the quiz was prepared, but don't read through the questions with them.

The activity is in four parts:

a Students work through the questions individually, giving **true** answers. The teacher should go round to help with any comprehension problems.

b Students compare their answers and discuss them. This stage should be fairly brief (maximum 5 minutes).

c Students work in pairs to decide which answers should earn top marks. They should make a separate note of these. The teacher should make sure they understand the instructions first.

You may like to have a brief feedback stage where students report back their selected answers and say why they have chosen them.

d Students then turn to the answer, page 217, and see whether they chose the right answers for the right reasons.

A further feedback stage may follow if there are any language points which the teacher has noted and would like to draw the students' attention to.

▶ Text 3 (p. 95)

1 Example answers

a He probably felt terrified.
b He was polite and friendly.
c He knew they had knives and suspected that they also had guns.
d He speaks in very simple English and also uses gestures.
e Because he was travelling cheaply by local boat rather than by air.
f They probably thought he would show fear.
g He wanted to please them and also to show that he admired them and was not afraid.
h They took fifty dollars. He explained that he would need the second note when he arrived at the next port.
i Yes, since Moros are known to kill the crew and passengers of boats sometimes.
j By being friendly and showing no fear.

2

a	snooping	*f*	bulges
b	clambered	*g*	took to be
c	stopped dead	*h*	mimed someone scribbling
d	edging	*i*	grinned
e	cautiously	*j*	exotic

3 Example answers

'Who are you? An American?' (line 9)
'No, I'm English. Are you from Tawitawi?' (line 10)
'I'm going to Zamboanga.' (line 16)
'Are you selling (anything)?' (17)
'No, I'm not selling (anything). I'm not a merchant. I'm a writer. I'm writing a book.' (18)
'Do you write magazines too?' (21)
'You must be very famous.' (23)
'No. I'm not famous. I'm a very poor man.' (24)
'So you're going in a kumpit, you're not going in an aeroplane.' (28/29)
'Moro people are very brave.' (33)
'Do English people say that? Do people in England know about Moros?' (34/35)
'Is that a Malaysian dollar? Will you show it to me, please?' (41)
'Will you give it to me?' (43)
'Yes, I'll give you that one. I'll keep this one. I need it for Zamboanga. Otherwise I'll have no money.' (45–47)
'Maybe someone will steal it.' (49/50)
'Yes. I carry very little money. Maybe pirates will come onto the kumpit. Are there any pirates here in the Sula Sea?' (51)
'My friends say that there are pirates here ... But Moros aren't pirates. Moros are fighting Marcos. Are you scared?' (55, 57/58)
'Scared? Why should I be scared?' (59)
'My name is Musa. What's you name?' (64/65)

Vocabulary included in Exam practice A: as if (8), experiment (9), limited (13), to spot (38), to tap (40), otherwise (47), shoulder *level* (61).

▶ Focus on grammar 2 · The past perfect (p. 96)

1

a they'd expected
b had spotted; I had forgotten
c he had done
d we had been riding

2

Present perfect simple		Present perfect continuous	
Had	+ past participle	Had	+ been + present participle
Hadn't		Hadn't	

3 The police didn't make any arrests because the thieves *had already left.*

If we used the past simple for both actions, it would mean that the thieves left *at the moment* when the police arrived. The numbers would reverse in that case.

```
        2              1
a  stopped        'd expected
        1              1          2
b  had spotted    had forgotten  tapped
        2              1
c  were           had done
        1              2
d  had been riding  came
```

Exercise 1

1 had just finished	11 had been dreaming
2 rang	12 decided
3 went	13 had mistaken
4 had told	14 noticed
5 opened	15 examined
6 saw	16 realised
7 I had heard	17 had pushed
8 had looked	18 had never seen
9 shut	19 began
10 began	

Exercise 2

a The examiner said that he hoped we had read the instructions carefully

b She explained that she wasn't sure she had found the answer to (my) question though she had spent a week thinking about it.

c He said he couldn't shake hands with me because his hands were oily and explained that he had been working on his car.

▶ Focus on listening 2 (p. 97)

Optional introduction

Write the headline from the Lead-in ('My lone walk to the North Pole') on the board and ask students to recall what they can about: the traveller's appearance, his method of travel, his equipment. (*Note*: They can turn to the picture on page 87 if their memories need jogging.)

Ask them what particular problems he mentioned in the short extract from a newspaper article. Elicit: poor visibility, radio and compass not working, feeling cold, tired, confused.

Ask the reason he gave for making the journey.

Ask what other methods of travel there are in the Arctic. Pre-teach: dog teams, snowmobiles, air support.

True/false

1 True.

2 False. ('I cracked three ribs and I gave up', 'I achieved about three-quarters of the distance')

3 True. ('everyone said ... I would be dead in six days ...')

4 False. ('every minute I hated it')

5 True. ('it was something that I had to get back to')

6 False

7 False. (He knew he was going through a migration route for polar bears, and he put Mars bars out at night because of that.)

8 True. ('I heard this rustling and this polar bear was after the Mars bar')

9 False. ('I shot a round through the floor just to scare it')

10 True. ('It really upset me ... It was a shame because they're such beautiful animals')

▶ Focus on writing · Formal letter (p. 98)

Layout

If necessary, refer students to the sample letter on page 222 of the Writing Bank.

```
                                        22 Green Lane

                                        Bath

                                        Avon

                                        June 8th 19-

The Project Director

Amazon Expedition

8 Bell Street

LONDON WC3 5YA


Dear Sir,




                      Yours faithfully,
```

Remind students *never* to put their name before the address, and to write the street, town and county or country on separate lines.

Remind them to write the date in full (ie *not* 8/6/19–) and to check abbreviations (Jan., Feb., etc. and 1st, 2nd, etc.)

Remind students of the Dear Sir ... Yours faithfully, Dear Mr X ... Yours sincerely, rule.

Remind them, too, to use capital 'Y' and small 's' or 'f', followed by a comma.

When this task has been completed and discussed, ask students to read each paragraph silently. Ask them to say what information each paragraph gives (for example, paragraph 1 gives the reason for writing the letter, with necessary information about which advertisement is referred to).

Draw students' attention to useful phrases such as 'I was very interested in ...', 'the advertisement in today's edition of ...', 'I look forward to hearing from you.'

Style

Unsuitable features of style include:

1 Abbreviations: for example, ad.

2 Colloquial expressions and slang: for example, fun, come along, About myself:, I couldn't stand, a bit of money, I didn't stick ..., come in handy, great, call in for a chat.

3 Ending: 'Yours' is only suitable in a personal letter.

4 General: The letter is too casual in its approach. The writer doesn't seem to think it's necessary to 'sell' himself in the right

way, and he isn't polite enough. (Ask students to compare the letter with the previous one.)

Describing objects

1 *a* (a saddle) It's made of leather (the stirrups are made of steel).
  b (a record) It's circular and made of plastic.
  c (a sweater) It's made of wool or nylon and it's spotted. The collar and sleeves are plain.
  d (a tie) It's made of silk/cotton etc. and striped.
  e (a set square) It's triangular and made of plastic.
  f (a table cloth) It's square or rectangular and made of checked cotton or linen.
  g (a mirror) It's oval and made of glass. (The frame is probably made of wood.)
  h (a chest of drawers) It's rectangular and made of wood.

2

long	*short*	expensive	*cheap*
hard	*soft*	enormous	*tiny*
heavy	*light*	curved	*straight*
thick	*thin*	dark (colours)	*light/pale*
smooth	*rough*	bright (colours)	*dull*
wide	*narrow*		
full	*empty*		
sharp	*blunt*		
tight	*loose*		
hollow	*solid*		

Writing task

Revise *strap*, *buckle*, *handle* and *catch* from Unit 1A, and any other relevant vocabulary that the students might need.

Go through the instructions and the plan with the class before setting the exercise for class or homework.

▶ Exam practice A · Vocabulary (p. 101)

1 *c* (Lead-in 3b)	14 *d* (2.8)
2 *d* (Lead-in 3b)	15 *c* (3.47)
3 *c* (Grammar 2)	16 *d* (Grammar 1)
4 *b* (1.35)	17 *b* (3.13)
5 *a* (1.8)	18 *c* (3.9)
6 *d* (1.21)	19 *a* (3.61)
7 *c* (1.20)	20 *d* (3.9)
8 *b* (Grammar 1)	21 *a* (3.40)
9 *d* (1.30/31)	22 *c* (Unit 1A Lead-in)
10 *d* (2.16)	23 *b* (Unit 1A Grammar 1)
11 *a* (2.14)	24 *a* (Unit 1A Study Box 1)
12 *b* (2.28)	25 *b* (3.38)
13 *a* (2.18)	

▶ Odd man out (p. 103)

Suggested answers

1 *tram* – the others are kinds of boats
  or *yacht* – not normally public transport
2 *tractor* – the only one with an engine
  or *sledge* – hasn't got wheels
3 *car* – a private vehicle, not a commercial one
4 *taxi* – not public transport/doesn't have a fixed route
5 *runway* – part of an airport; the others are to do with rail transport
6 *conductor* – doesn't have control of a vehicle
  or *cyclist* – his or her vehicle has no engine
7 *platform* – part of a station; the others are to do with ships
8 *station* – the others are to do with bus transport
9 *goat* – the only animal not used to pull vehicles
10 *Cairo* – not a sea port

Notes

There may well be other possible answers, and, if these are satisfactorily argued by students, they should of course be accepted.

All the vocabulary from this exercise and others like it in the book is included in the *Cambridge English Lexicon*, a word list used by those who prepare Cambridge examination materials.

Take the opportunity to revise and expand students' topic vocabulary by checking the meaning of all the items and explaining/illustrating those they don't know.

UNIT 2B Family life

▶Lead-in (p. 104)

1 The two photographs provide further practice for the Picture Conversation part of Paper 5 in the examination, the Interview.

A good way of making this a more interesting activity, and of providing useful practice in asking questions, is to follow the procedure for the 'Witness' communication activity in Unit 4A.

Students work in pairs: Student A studies the first picture for 30–60 seconds and then closes the book. Student B then asks questions about the picture to see how much detail Student A remembers. The procedure is then reversed as Student B studies the second picture and is questioned in turn.

Afterwards, ask pairs to report back on any mistakes or omissions that were made, and give students the chance to ask for specific vocabulary items that they want to know. Take the opportunity to revise vocabulary relating to appearance and clothing, as necessary.

2 Questionnaire

Allow students time to read through the 12 statements and to ask any questions they may have before they start. The following may need checking/explanation:

1 financial support
2 the family budget
3 to share *fairly*
8 to have the last word
9 to respect a person's wishes (*Note*: The meaning here is probably 'to consider seriously, but not necessarily to follow'.)

When students have finished discussing their answers in pairs, open up a class discussion, asking students to give reasons for their opinions.

Vocabulary included in Exam practice A: to share *between* two people (*among* more than two).

▶Text 1 · A really equal partner (p. 105)

2 True/false

a False. ('John … cooks the evening meal twice a week')
b False. (When he was a child, they all mucked in.)
c True. ('John does occasionally resent …')
d False. ('being with the children is just more important ..')
e True. ('John's responsible for about 60 to 70 percent')
f False. ('Pam … not to be too concerned … housework.')
g True. ('… the boys look to her more than to him for affection.')
h False. ('Pam and I are very different people.')

3 Vocabulary matching

a throws a minor fit
b have it all taped
c mucking in
d by no means
e chores
f cuddle (and mumsy)
g better off
h an uphill struggle
i mod cons
j a throwback

Multiple-choice

4 *b*
5 *c*
6 *d*
7 *b*
8 *a*

Vocabulary included in Exam practice A: to reduce (27), to suit/well-suited (33), a person's *turn* (44), concerned *about* (52), despite (67), to *make* an effort (79), to have views *on* (85).

▶Focus on grammar 1 · The infinitive (p. 107)

Exercise 1 (Example answers)

a to lose weight
b to design our house
c to report the burglary
d to mend the washing machine
e to tell him about my headaches
f to put out the fire
g to see the world
h To win the match

Exercise 2

a simple to use
b disappointed to hear
c anxious to know
d certain to be
e hard to believe
f delighted to meet
g amazed to see
h important to check

Exercise 3 (Example answers)

a to lift
b to make an omelette
c to take off/land
d to sail
e to read the notice
f to take your driving test

Exercise 4 (Example answers)

a persuade him
b prefer to have
c happen to
d remind me to
e forbade me to
f afford to buy
g advised me to
h want/hope to
i help you to
j told you not to

Exercise 5

1 worrying
2 to spend
3 having
4 to stay
5 to look after
6 taking
7 to be
8 to arrange
9 combining
10 running
11 bringing up
12 to get
13 to buy
14 driving
15 get
16 to take
17 to get
18 travelling
19 staying
20 to get

▶Communication activity (p. 108)

Follow the procedure for the similar communication activity in Unit 5A (page 63).

This time students should be able to find all ten differences without looking at the pictures together.

Differences

1 Flag (A: horizontal stripes; B: vertical stripes)
2 Shells on sandcastle (A: two; B: one)
3 Bucket next to man (A: upright; B: upside down)
4 Swimsuit (A: green with white spots; B: white with green spots)
5 Object near woman's foot (A: crab; B: starfish)
6 Book cover (A: heart shape; B: triangle)
7 Bottle (A: behind deckchair; B: beside deckchair)
8 Ship (A: pointing to the right; B: pointing to the left)
9 Shark (in picture A only)
10 Glasses on picnic hamper (A: sunglasses; B: ordinary glasses)

Checking

Ask students to describe each difference accurately and check/teach the necessary vocabulary.

Check/teach any other useful vocabulary (for example, *spade, yacht, beachball*).

▶Focus on listening 1 · Children speaking (p. 109)

Give students time to read the instructions and the information given in the table. Check vocabulary as necessary (for example, *pocket money, punishment, lay the table, wipe up, a smack*).

	Age	Brothers/ Sisters	Pocket Money	Spends Pocket Money on . . .	Help in the house	Punishment	Bed Time Earliest	Bed Time Latest
First Child	9	2 brothers	£3.50	Sweets	washing up and laying the table.	gets sent to bed or gets a smack.	9.30pm	11pm
Second Child	7	1 brother 1 sister	50p	sweets	washing up, dusting, wiping up + putting things away.	gets sent to bed	8 or 9pm	10pm
Third Child	8	(none)	£1 - £2	toys	lay the table and bring the knives and forks.	gets a smack	8pm	11pm

Discussion points

1 Ask students to report back about what their partner said.
2 Open up a class discussion and invite as many opinions as possible.

▶ Text 2 · Working mothers: what children say (p. 109)

Note: Explain *neglect* beforehand, if necessary.

1 Suggested answers

a Because the family had just moved to a new town and Debbie had just started at a new school where she had to make new friends.
b She didn't like her ('I couldn't stand her') because she was a nuisance.
c She liked being trusted with her own key and she enjoyed feeling independent.
d No she doesn't. Her mother always had time for her. (lines 20–24)
e She learnt how to look after herself and how to run a house which she is finding useful in her adult life.

Note: You may prefer to do the vocabulary exercise (6) now, before going on to the next text.

3 Suggested answers

a He dislikes coming home to an empty house.
b She agreed to try the new arrangement for a short period to see how the family liked it and she said she would give up her job if they were unhappy.
c In some ways he does. He would obviously like his mother to be there to welcome him when he comes home from school. He also mentions that people were more interested in his mother's new job than in his experiences at his new school. On the other hand, his mother tells him interesting things, takes him on holidays abroad and gives him money for his hobbies.
d He gets extra pocket money; he has more freedom; there is more money for holidays and hobbies; his mother has interesting stories to tell.
e No, he doesn't. (lines 36–37)

Note: You may prefer to do the vocabulary exercise (7) now before going on to the true/false questions.

5 True/false

Note: Some statements (particularly a and f) may be either true or false, depending on the argument.

a False. (Debbie's sister was younger and got in her way. Peter's sister is older than him and busy studying.)
b False. (Peter found it exciting in the beginning.)
c True.
d False.
e True.
f False. (Debbie does; Peter doesn't.)
g True.
h False. (He didn't think it was a fair test.)

6
a	a	
b	c	
c	c	
d	b	
e	b	
f	a	

7
a trial
b thrilling
c long term
d mow
e get round to
f told off
g swap

Discussion points

Either ask students to work in pairs or small groups, or treat this as class discussion.

Vocabulary included in Exam practice A: 1st text: wear off (18), trust (18); 2nd text: interested in (19), fair (26).

▶ Focus on grammar 2 · Reporting statements (p. 111)

Exercise 1

a His wife complained that he never lifted a finger to help her.
b My father promised to give me a hand with my homework that evening.
c I explained that I was late because the bus had broken down.
d My friend admitted that he had had an accident with my car.
e The teacher argued that John ought to go first because he was the youngest.

Exercise 2

a The interviewer asked him to shut the door.
b My mother reminded me to switch off the fire.
c The receptionist invited me to sit down and wait.
d My friend advised me to lie down.
e My boss forbade me to tell anyone about the product.
f The gunman warned them not to move or he would shoot.
g Some friends of mine recommended me to stay at the Imperial Hotel (if I could).

Exercise 3 (Suggested answers)

a to sit in
b that his car was in a
c to play
d that I had passed
e not to make
f to drive carefully
g to feed
h to try
i that the library was/would be
j not to go to Morocco in July

Exercise 4

Debbie said that since she had got married the previous June, she had appreciated the extra independence that had come from looking after herself for part of the day. She said she knew what things cost because she was used to shopping and she knew how much work went into running a house. She explained that a lot of girls she had grown up with, who had never learned to fend for themselves, must have come down to earth with a bump. She finished by saying that when she had children she hoped she could do as well as her mother, but she didn't know if she would have enough patience and energy.

▶ Focus on writing 1 · Informal letter (p. 113)

Revise the main points of layout and style (Unit 2A, p. 28/29; Writing Bank, p. 220).

It's useful to have a planning phase during a class. Students should make notes for the various paragraphs of their letters, and these can be checked before they go on to write the complete letter.

Another useful exercise is to ask students to exchange their finished letters and to correct each other's work, as far as they are able. They can then return the letters and point out the mistakes they have spotted. This provides more immediate feedback than the teacher can usually give, focuses on accuracy, requires informal oral communication *and* tends to encourage the students to 'proof-read' their own work more carefully!

▶ Focus on listening 2 · Single parent family (p. 113)

Give students time to read through the questions and to ask any questions they may have before beginning the exercise.

True/false

1 False. (They separated 3 years ago.)
2 True. (a 13-year-old daughter and a 5-year-old son)
3 True. ('a very good supportive group of women friends' who 'share the child care')
4 False. (her mother-*in-law*)

5 True.

6 False. (He's in quite good health, so she only needs to visit him once every four weekends to see if he's OK.)

7 True. ('I get some help. I don't think it's enough really. I think … fathers get off rather lightly.')

8 False. (They see him once a week.)

9 women

10 6 months

11 nothing

12 independent

Discussion points

These can be discussed in pairs, small groups, or by the class as a whole. You might even like students to give answers in writing, for homework, following the discussion.

Vocabulary included in Exam practice A: mind + ing

▶ **Focus on grammar 3 · Comparatives: The … the …** (p. 114)

Exercise 1 (Example answers)

a The more exercise you take, the *fitter* you will become.

b The *bigger* the car, the *more expensive* it is to hire.

c The *more slowly* you speak, the *easier* it is for me to understand.

d The *more* you study, *the greater (the)* chance you will have in the exam.

e *The better* I get to know him, *the less* I like him, I'm sorry to say.

f The more frightening the film, *the more he enjoys it.*

g The sharper the knife, *the easier it is to cut with.*

h *The longer I stayed away*, the more homesick I felt.

Exercise 2 (Example answers)

a The more I earn, the happier I'll be. *or* The more money you have, the less contented you'll be.

b The older you get, the wiser you become.

▶ **Focus on writing 2 · Directed writing** (p. 115)

Introduce the topic by asking students which places they would suggest in the local area as suitable for a family outing.

Ask students to look quickly at the four sections to say what the four places are. Check *aquarium* and *watermill* if necessary.

1 Ask students to answer questions *a–g*. They should check their answers together when they finish.

a 3 – waterfalls and river walks; 4 – river, wooded valley

b 4 – pigs, goats etc.

c 1 – café; 3 – refreshments; 4 – fresh baked bread and pastries

d 1 – gift and bookshop; (3 – the shop might sell souvenirs)

e 3 – special arrangements for groups and schools; (2 – pre-arranged groups might include school groups)

f 2 (though not over Christmas itself); 3 (but limited services)

g 1, 2, 3

2 Suggested procedure

Ask students to read the information about the family members and to write the numbers of places which have something to offer next to the texts. For example, they should write the number 4 next to both Colin and Carol White, since Felin Geri is a historical building and offers cookery demonstrations.

When students have finished, they should be able to see which is the best choice for the whole family from the number which occurs most frequently.

If you feel that it is necessary, go through the notes for the first paragraph with the class, to make sure they include all the relevant information. You may even want to compose the first paragraph with the class's help, as an example.

Encourage students to use their own words, as far as possible.

Note: The example answers below are not the only 'right' ones and other choices are possible if well enough argued.

1 The best choice for the whole family would be Felin Geri because it has something to offer for everybody. Colin would be interested in the old watermill as a historical building and he and his wife would be able to walk in the beautiful Ceri Valley. The cookery demonstrations would appeal to Carol, and their children would love to see all the farm animals. Finally, their grandmother could enjoy the scenery too.

2 Another good choice would be the Aberaeron Aquarium, which has plenty to interest the family, including an entertainment video. As it is very close to the beach, it would certainly be popular with the children. There's a bookshop which should appeal to Colin and Carol and, since the aquarium and shop are on one level, it would also be suitable for Mrs Carter, who can't walk very easily.

3 They might not all enjoy the Talyllyn Railway because, although the children would probably love the train ride, they might find that they were sharing the carriage with a party of noisy schoolchildren and Mrs Carter wouldn't like that at all! Colin and Carol could take the children for walks in the countryside nearby, but they would have to leave Mrs Carter on her own in the meantime.

4 I wouldn't recommend them to visit the Museum of the Woollen Industry because, although the collection of machinery and tools is extensive and the exhibition of photographs is probably very interesting, it is less likely to appeal to everyone, and the children, in particular, might get bored. Mrs Carter might find that there was too much walking involved. There don't seem to be any other attractions such as attractive scenery, a café or a shop.

▶ **Exam practice A · Vocabulary** (p. 116)

1 *b* (1.85)

2 *d* (2, Debbie. 13)

3 *b* (2, Debbie. 20)

4 *d* (1.44)

5 *c* (1.79, Unit 2A Study Box 2)

6 *b* (1.67)

7 *a* (1, Debbie. 18)

8 *a* (1.27)

9 *d* (2, Peter. 13 & 27)

10 *c* (2, Debbie. 10)

11 *d* (1.52)

12 *a* (2, Debbie. 17)

16 *c* (1.33)

17 *a* (Focus on writing, introduction)

18 *b* (Focus on grammar 1)

19 *d* (Focus on writing 2, Text 1)

20 *a* (2, Peter. 19)

21 *c* (Focus on writing 2, Text 4)

22 *c* (Unit 2A Focus on grammar 1)

23 *b* (Focus on writing 2,

UNIT **3B** Looking after yourself

▶ Lead-in 1 · What is health? (p. 118)

Questionnaire

Ask the students to read through the 14 statements fairly quickly and to tell you if there are any words or expressions which they don't understand.

Draw their attention to 'out of breath', 'hardly ever' and 'a *mild* stomach upset' and check understanding.

When everyone has chosen their five statements (and ticked the first column), ask them to compare their results with one or (preferably) two other students and to write **their** results in the second column. Encourage them to discuss their reasons and to ask each other questions.

Feedback

Rather than work through all the students or all the statements, which can kill the interest in the topic, concentrate on common or uncommon answers:

Ask which numbers were chosen by all the members of each group, and see if there is any agreement across the class. If there is, do reasons correspond too?

Ask which numbers were only chosen by one member of each group and ask for reasons.

Passages

Allow students time to read each passage silently. At this stage, you may like to ask a student who has chosen one or more of the numbers mentioned to read a passage aloud. This skill is no longer tested in the examination, however.

Discuss the points raised. For example:
(Passage 1) How could you be fit and still be unhealthy?
(Passage 2) Why is it that doctors can do little to help us to be healthy?
(Passage 3) Is it worth living to be very old if you don't enjoy life?
(Passage 4) What can we do to encourage positive health?

Vocabulary included in Exam practice A: out of *breath*, *hardly* ever, a *mild* cold.

▶ Lead-in 2 · Changing times (p. 119)

Matching exercise
2, 4, 1, 3 (numbers in boxes)

▶ Text 1 (p. 120)

Note: Ask the students to read and answer the True/false questions **before** they read Text 1. This provides a strong motivation to read the text in order to see they were right or not.

Discuss answers (without judging them right or wrong) briefly before asking students to read the text.

1 True/false
a True. ('If you go on eating … your health will suffer.')
b True. ('The tendency to put on weight … runs in families.')
c True. ('Your upbringing shapes some basic attitudes … a sweet tooth.')
d False. ('You're more likely to put on weight … if you're a woman.')
e False. ('We eat about twice as much protein as we need.')
f True. ('It is a waste of time and money to take vitamin pills.')
g False. ('Don't make the mistake of thinking … energetic.')
h False. ('Food with plenty of fibre … too many calories.')

2
a efficient	d cope	g determine	j nibble
b extracting	e eventually	h shape	k alter
c huge	f inherit	i upbringing	l striking

3 Describing food

Spicy	Bitter	Salty	Sweet	Sour	Greasy	Creamy
curry	olives beer almonds coffee (black)	peanuts anchovies crisps	honey ice cream peaches bananas	lemon vinegar grapefruit	fish and chips sausages	butter ice cream yoghurt onion soup

Note: Tastes differ! Other classifications are possible, within reason.

Optional writing exercise

Write two paragraphs, one describing your favourite dish and one describing the dish you think is most unpleasant.

Vocabulary included in Exam practice A: (references are to numbered **parts** of Text 1) not *counting* (1), depend *on* (1), *put on* weight (1,2), upbringing/to bring up (2), attitude *to/towards* (2), to alter (2), raw (4), varied (4), unless (4), in comparison *with* (6).

▶ Focus on listening 1 · Old wives' tales? (p. 122)

It is helpful to give an example of an old wives' tale that students might be familiar with. Check that students are quite clear about the meaning of this phrase before proceeding.

Ask students to guess whether the five old wives' tales given are true, partly true, or false, and to discuss their opinions with one or two other students. Don't confirm or deny their answers at this stage!

Check the meaning of tales 1 and 4 in particular and explain if necessary. Tale 1: Eating an apple every day will keep you healthy so that you don't need to see a doctor. Tale 4: Have plenty to eat when you've got a cold but don't eat anything if you've got a high temperature.

Part A
1 Partly true (an exaggeration).
2 False (dangerous for old people and babies).
3 False (no evidence).
4 True.
5 True (contains Vitamin A, which enables the eye to adapt to the dark).

Part B
1 An orange.
2 Old people and babies.
3 He fell into a freezing river (during the spring thaw).
4 To drink plenty of liquid (to replace fluid lost through sweating).
5 Green beans, milk, butter, fish oils.

Vocabulary included in Exam practice A: to suffer *from*, recommend (somebody) *to do* (something).

▶ Focus on grammar 1 · Expressing quantity (p. 122)

a

Countable		Uncountable	
biscuit vitamin apple snack plate	coin chair programme journey	rice spaghetti crockery news travel music	money blood information weather furniture

b
chocolate	(i)	a sweet
	(ii)	food substance
time	(i)	an occasion
	(ii)	the passing of days etc.
wood	(i)	a group of trees
	(ii)	material
hair	(i)	a single piece of hair
	(ii)	all the hairs on one's head

iron   (i) an instrument for smoothing clothes
       (ii) material

tin   (i) a container
      (ii) material

exercise (i) an activity to train the body
       (ii) activity in general

skin   (i) an animal hide
      (ii) the substance which covers the body

Countable	Uncountable	Both	
too few very many a great many A large number of	too much a large amount of very little a great deal of	a lot of hardly any not enough	no ... at all plenty of a lack of

Exercise 1

1 how much
2 little
3 no applause at all
4 lack
5 not enough/too few

6 number
7 plenty of/a lot of
8 deal of
9 hardly any/very little
10 many

Exercise 2

a Bristol has twice as many inhabitants as Southampton.
b The first camera costs five times as much as the second.
c It's nearly twice as hot in Athens today as it is in London.
d The trains from London to Brighton are three times as frequent as those from London to Swansea.
e Mount Everest is more than six times as high as Ben Nevis.
f Concorde is ten times as fast as a BMW.

▶ Communication activity (The Laughing Cook restaurant) (p. 124)

Preparation

Decide beforehand which roles students will have. The role of A is probably most suitable for stronger students. If the class doesn't divide evenly into threes, the extra one or two students can act as observers. They should be told privately that they will be asked to report back on what they've seen.

Let students read the introduction and menu on page 124 (tell them not to turn to the instructions for each role yet). Check that they know what they have to do and answer any questions about vocabulary they may want to ask.

Tell each student whether he/she is A, B or Waiter.

Ask all the waiters to form a group at the side of the class for a few minutes. They should read and discuss their instructions. Tell them privately to decide what to say when they go to take an order and also to discuss what they can say in order to persuade the customers to order the three dishes which the chef wants to get rid of. (You can suggest they look at the Functions Bank on page 209.)

Ask the A and B students to sit together as if they were in a restaurant. This will work much better if they can sit facing each other across a table, even if it means a bit of moving about to achieve the arrangement. Ask them to turn to their instructions and read them but **not** to show each other!

Role play

Check that each pair has decided on their relationship and then let the activity begin.

Allow about 5 minutes' conversation before telling the waiters to approach their customers. Meanwhile tour round and listen in, making your presence felt as little as possible. Note down any language difficulties.

Feedback

As each group finishes, let them look at each other's instructions. When everyone has finished, ask each group to report back briefly on what dishes were chosen and why. Ask them to say how persuasive A and the Waiter were, and ask any observers for their comments.

(Optional) Refer students to the Functions Bank on page 209 and practise as necessary. Deal with any language difficulties that you have noted.

▶ Focus on grammar 2 · Reported questions (p. 125)

'Excuse me, *where is the post office?*'
She asked me how my parents *were.*
They wanted to know who I *had gone home with.*

Exercise 1

a ...how much I earned.
b ...where I had bought my watch.
c ...how many kilos I had lost.
d ...when I was coming/going to stay with her.
e ...why she wouldn't marry him.
f ...who on earth had given him my address.
I asked if you *liked jazz.*
He asked if he *could use the telephone.*

Exercise 2

a ...if I had (got) change of a £5 note.
b ...if I had seen Tim that day.
c ...would be at home that weekend.
d ...if my wife spoke any Portuguese.
e ...if I had telephoned her the previous night.
f ...if I could lend him £1 till the following day.

Exercise 4

a ...what the capital of Australia is?
b ...what the language spoken in Holland is?
c ...what the unit of currency in Japan is?
d ...who the President of France is?
e ...where the nearest bank is?
f ...when the next First Certificate examination is/will be?
g ...what time it is?
h ...where the last Olympic Games were (held)?
i ...what the word 'dawn' means?
j ...how long the course lasts?

▶ Text 2 · Cuts, bruises, bites, burns (p. 126)

A possible lead-in would be to draw a cross (like the Red Cross symbol) on the board and ask students what it would mean if they found that sign in red on a white box. When would they need to use the contents of the box and why? Elicit from the students some names of minor injuries (for example, *nose bleed, black eye, twisted ankle*) and ask what treatments they would recommend.

1 a Plaster and bandage are not minor injuries.
  b (From left to right) burn, scald, plaster, bruise, cut, bandage, bite (but bee's/wasp's *sting*), graze.

2 Allow 2–3 minutes' reading time and then ask students to answer the questions.
  1 d (Check why the other options are wrong:
    a – It is not always necessary for a doctor to come;
    b – We *know* what causes minor illnesses;
    c – Not always, for example if the patient has been knocked out.
  2 c ('leave the graze uncovered. Exposure to the air ...')
  3 b ('Bleeding can ... be stopped by applying pressure)
  4 a (by avoiding long exposure and covering exposed areas)
  5 b (The *limb* should be raised. Lying in bed is the easiest way to do this.)

Vocabulary included in Exam practice A: bite/bitten.

▶ Focus on listening 2 (p. 128)

Explain that students are going to hear part of a talk about First Aid. Give them time to read through the questions and ask about any vocabulary they don't know.

Multiple-choice

1 *d* (One afternoon a week for a total of 20 hours.)
2 *a* ('You can be a more effective first aider if you're prepared … to do some extra practice at home.')
3 *c* (He was purple.)
4 *d* ('Lying across the chair … facing the floor')
5 *c* ('sometimes people get terrified in this kind of situation.')
6 *a* ('something … blocking his airway')
7 *d* (They took him off anyway because he needed to be medically examined.)
8 *b* (You've got to recognise what sort of situation it is and, if it's an emergency, act very, very quickly.)

▶ **Focus on grammar 3 · Expressing number** (p. 129)

Exercise

1 both
2 Every
3 none
4 each
5 all
6 Neither
7 either
8 all
9 neither
10 either, Both

▶ **Focus on writing · Directed writing** (p. 130)

(Optional) The two pictures can be used for practising descriptions for the first part of Paper 5 in the examination (Interview). Encourage students to make full use of the information in the pictures and to use the language of speculation.

Ask students to read through the instructions and the two paragraphs and tell them to underline the points which they need to bear in mind when choosing a suitable sport for the two people. They should then make brief notes, for example:

Sue Adam – wants regular exercise to regain fitness
– not expensive
– preferably in the open air and with the opportunity of developing a skill

Chris Williams – needs exercise to lose weight
– opportunity to meet people
– not a competitive sport
– not needing much skill

Ask students to read through the notes on five sports. Deal with any vocabulary problems, such as *coaching, tees, waistline*.

Example answers

1 In my opinion, the sport which would suit both Sue Adam and Chris Williams is swimming because it would be a good way for both of them to get fit. Sue would be able to learn a skill such as diving or life saving, while Chris could make friends if he joined a club. They wouldn't have to travel far or spend much money, but an outdoor pool would be preferable for Sue.

2 Other sports Sue Adam could consider would be tennis or cycling. She would get plenty of exercise with tennis and could develop her skill, as long as she could afford to pay for coaching. Cycling would be cheaper and enjoyable (provided she owns a bike), but it wouldn't provide much opportunity to develop a skill.

3 Another good choice for Chris Williams would be cycling or jogging. Cycling doesn't need much skill, and jogging needs none, yet they're both very good exercise. If he took up either sport, he would have the opportunity of joining a club so he could meet people and make new friends.

4 The sport which would be unsuitable for both Sue Adam and Chris Williams is golf. It would be less effective exercise for them than the other activities, and it would be too expensive for Sue Adam to take up because of the equipment she would have to buy. Chris Williams would enjoy the social life of the golf club, but drinking in the bar or eating in the restaurant might ruin all his efforts at losing weight!

▶ **Exam practice A · Vocabulary** (p. 131)

(References are to numbered parts of texts.)

1 *c* (Lead-in 1,3)
2 *a* (1,1)
3 *d*
4 *c* (Lead-in 1,2)
5 *b* (1,4)
6 *a* (1,5)
7 *b* (1.2, Unit 1B Study Box 3)
8 *d* (1,4)
9 *c* (2)
10 *a* (1,3)
11 *c* (2)
12 *b* (1,1,2)
13 *d* (Lead-in 1,6)
14 *c* (1,6)
15 *a* (1,2)
16 *c* (Listening 1, Study Box 1)
17 *b* (Listening 1, Study Box 2)
18 *c* (Listening 1, Unit 2B, Focus on grammar 1 & 2, Functions Bank)
19 *c* (Focus on grammar 1)
20 *d* (Focus on grammar 1)
21 *d* (1, 1)
22 *a* (Unit 3A, Focus on grammar 2)
23 *b* (Functions Bank)
24 *a* (Functions Bank)
25 *d* (Unit 3A, Study Box 3)

▶ **Odd man out** (p. 133)

For general notes on this type of exercise, see Unit 1B, page 27.

1 *thumb* – the others are parts of the face.
2 *ribbon* – not used for medical purposes.
3 *stomach* – the others are joints.
4 *spot* – the others are injuries.
5 *eggs* – the others are products made from milk (dairy products).
6 *boil* – the only method of cooking which uses water.
7 *chips* – the others are uncountable.
or *meat* – the only animal product.
8 *ironmonger's* – the others are food shops.
9 *judo* – not a ball game.
10 *Sydney* – the others have held Olympic Games.

UNIT **4B** Narrow escapes

▶Lead-in (p. 134)

2 1 *i, e*
  2 *c, d, h*
  3 *a, f*
  4 *b, g*
  Ask students to explain which order the extracts should come in and which words helped them to match the extracts to the headlines.

3 Get students to explain the four narrow escapes to each other and/or the whole class. Let them re-read the extracts, encouraging them to *guess* any unknown vocabulary, for example, (*a*) an electrical appliance, to be mystified, dressing table.

Note: The Language check exercise on page 136 includes a number of prepositional phrases from these extracts.

4 Example answers

Although the child fell from a moving car on to the road, he was completely unhurt. It was as if he had been made of rubber and bounced like a ball.

The family have experienced two major accidents in their home in a short period of time. It seems that they are unusually unlucky.

Vocabulary included in Exam practice A: a second major accident *in* three months (*c*), otherwise (*e*), cause something *to happen* (*f*).

▶Text 1 · Jumbo nightmare (p. 135)

1 *a* A dust cloud.
  b The engines stopped and the plane dived.
  c The captain managed to restart all four engines and to land the plane safely.

2 *a* That the plane was out of control.
  b The cabin filled with ash and smoke.
  c He saw an engine which seemed to be on fire.
  d The oxygen masks dropped down and the emergency signs lit up.
  e When the plane was diving.
  f After falling 25,000 feet when the plane came out of the bottom of the dust cloud.
  g The landing lights weren't working.
  h He said it was the result of his training and following instructions.
  i The plane was very badly damaged but had continued to fly.

3 *a* intercom   *f* cramped
  b distress   *g* an eternity
  c stricken   *h* turbulence
  d plunged   *i* starved of
  e an understatement   *j* disabled

4 Language check – prepositions
  a at (Extract *a*, Text 1, line 25), for (Extract *b*)
  b on (Extract *d*), to (Extract *h*)
  c in (Extract *c*)
  d at (Extract *b*)
  e into (Extract *i*)
  f in (Extract *i*)
  g in (Extract *i*)
  h on (Text 1, line 20)
  i with (Text 1, line 10)
  j up (Text 1, line 27).

Vocabulary included in Exam practice A: do one's best (7), out of action (14), on fire (21), to choke (32), due to (38), to *follow* instructions (38).

▶Focus on grammar 1 · Expressing time (p. 137)

Exercise 1

Same time	Later	Sequence
(even) as	It was not until	at first
at the same time	By the time …	finally
	When (it was all over)	

Special points (Example answers)
  a during the performance
    while he's having a bath
    lay the table, please?
  b first studied all the brochures.
    It was cloudy at first
  c when spring came at last
  d we went to a Chinese restaurant
    we went out for a meal

Exercise 2
  1 at first   7 then/next
  2 after   8 finally
  3 during   9 afterwards
  4 while   10 meanwhile
  5 before   11 at last
  6 first (ly)

Exercise 3 (Example answers)
  a gets/arrives   *e* arrive/have arrived at
  b come to live in   *f* I'm driving to
  c I've obtained a   *g* take the examination
  d he's on/he's caught the   *h* see/have seen

▶Communication activity 1 (p. 138)

Allow students to read through the text and explain any vocabulary that is unknown. It is also worth pointing out that foxes don't eat grain!

Tell students to work in pairs or small groups and to rearrange furniture as necessary.

Monitor their work but don't worry if they are not making great use of sequence markers at this stage.

If one student works out the answer quickly, make sure s/he explains it clearly to his/her partner or the rest of the group.

Ask students to take it in turns to explain the answer, one step at a time. Insist that they include sequence markers in their explanation now.

The answer is as follows:

First the man rows to dry land with the chicken, and returns. **Next** he rows across with the fox, and returns with the chicken to the house. **After that** he takes the grain to dry land and returns. **Finally**, he rows across with the chicken.

▶Focus on listening 1 · A survival kit (p. 139)

Check that students know the names for the various objects illustrated. Check their understanding of *survival kit* and ask them when such a thing would be useful.

1 (*a*) matchbox
  (*b*) nylon
  (*c*) fishing hook
  (*d*) carry water
  (*e*) there are no holes in it.
  (*f*) candle
  (*g*) stretch it too much
  (*h*) , to fish
  (*i*) waterproof
  (*j*) to write messages
  (*k*) whistle

2 9

3 11

Vocabulary included in Exam practice A: burst, so as to (see also Study Box 2).

▶ Focus on writing 1 · Instructions (p. 139)

1 *a* 5   4
       2   1
       7   6
            3

b 3 Place the head of a match in the wax and turn it carefully in order to *cover it completely.*

7 Lay the matches end to end so that *no two matches can touch.*

c **Example answer**
Be careful not to get hot wax on your fingers (after 2). Make sure you have sealed them completely (after 6). Once you have done that, (to link any two sentences).

d **Example answer**
Making matches waterproof
First, light a candle. Next, hold the candle over the base of the match box and let some wax drip into the base. Be careful not to get any hot wax on your fingers while you're doing this. Then place the head of a match in the wax and turn it carefully in order to cover it completely. Once you've done that, lay the match in the wax and drip wax along the length of the match. Then repeat the process for each match, making sure that they are completely sealed. Lay the matches end to end so that no two heads can touch.

2 Read through the short introduction on the fact sheet and make sure students understand what a solar still is, and what it does.

Check the details on the diagram and encourage students to use purpose clauses from the Study Box below. For example:

Why does the stone have to be smooth?
So that it doesn't tear the plastic sheet.

Check relevant items from the Functions Bank for expressing location. For example:

Where are the stones placed?
On either side of the hole.

Where is the smooth stone placed?
In the middle of the plastic sheet, *over* the container.

Example answer
First you need to choose a suitable place for your solar still. This should be in a low area and in full sunlight, otherwise it will not work. Then use your digging tool to make a hole in the ground which is about one metre deep and one metre across. After that, place a container such as a pan at the bottom in order to collect the water. Next, stretch the plastic sheet across the top of the hole and use some heavy stones to weigh it down on either side. Finally, choose a smooth stone and place it in the centre of the plastic sheet so that the sheet hangs down over the container. When you have done that, your solar still is now finished and you only have to wait for the results.

The sun will heat the air in the hole, and water will condense on the underside of the plastic sheet. Drops of water will form and will run down and fall into the container.

▶ Text 2 · Rescue from the rapids (p. 141)

Focus questions – example answers

1 Because he was carried away by the strong current and could have been drowned or smashed against the rocks.

2 Leon.

3 He was in a very bad state, unable to breathe properly and shaking.

Multiple-choice

4 *d* ('he lost his footing')

5 *a* ('snatching his left hand in my right')
6 *c* ('impossibly trying to grip . . . a smooth and shiny rock')
7 *c* ('launched himself . . . into the centre of the whirpool')
8 *b*

Vocabulary included in Exam practice A: let go of (3), current (6), slippery (11), to squeeze (21).

▶ Focus on grammar 2 · Modal verbs 4: Certainty/probability/possibility (p. 142)

1 Let students discuss their ideas about the picture in pairs first. The chances are that they won't use modal verbs to do this!

When you ask them to report back their ideas, draw their attention to the tables below and ask them to use that language. They should also be encouraged to disagree, using the negative: 'No, it can't be an African hut' etc.

The 'answer' is shown on page 218, but you may prefer to delay revealing this till later in the lesson.

Practice
This exercise can be extended if students can suggest other examples of their own.

Exercise 1

a My mother may (might/could) have phoned while we were out.
b Helen might (may) have seen the film on TV last night.
c You must have eaten too much at lunch.
d I can't have woken the baby, . . .
e John could (might/may) have forgotten the appointment in his diary.
f A pipe must have burst while we were away.
g The cleaning lady might (could/may) have thrown your cheque book away by mistake.

▶ Communication activity 2 · Brain-teasers (p. 144)

This activity is designed to provide freer practice in the use of the modal verbs which were presented in the previous grammar section. No introduction is needed, but students should be organised in pairs or small groups as necessary.

Monitor students' work and be prepared to help with any questions about vocabulary. Encourage them to use modal verbs for probability, but do this as unobtrusively as possible.

Afterwards, ask students who are confident that they have discovered the answers to explain them to the rest of the class. Deal with any language problems which arose.

A The car had gone into a river (or lake) and sunk to the bottom. The man had managed to escape by opening the window and then the car door, and swimming to the surface.
B He touched him, because he was in the boat with Dan.
C One train went through the tunnel at 2p.m. and the other went through at 3p.m.
D He saw him. It was daylight.

▶ Focus on listening 2 (p. 144)

Give students time to read through the questions and to look at the map. Check particularly that they understand the items in the key to the map.

Multiple-choice

1 *c*	3 *d*	5 *a*	7 *d*
2 *c*	4 *b*	6 *b*	

8

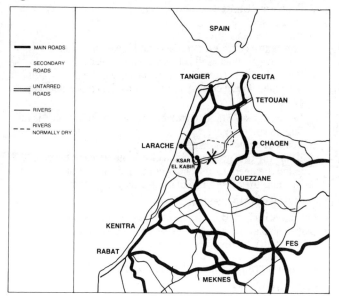

- MAIN ROADS
- SECONDARY ROADS
- UNTARRED ROADS
- RIVERS
- - - RIVERS NORMALLY DRY

▶ Focus on grammar 3 · Question tags (p. 146)

Note: It is useful to do this section immediately, or fairly soon, after Focus on listening 2.

Exercise 1

a	6	*f*	4
b	5	*g*	10
c	9	*h*	1
d	7	*i*	3
e	2	*j*	8

Special points

It may also be worth mentioning the special use of question tags where an affirmative tag follows an affirmative statement, or a negative one follows a negative statement. For example:

So you *refuse* to give me my money back, *do you*?
You *won't tell* me where you've been, *won't you*?

These patterns usually imply a particular emotion or attitude. They are often ironic or threatening in tone.

Exercise 2

a	didn't we?	*f*	should you?
b	have you?	*g*	didn't we?
c	wouldn't you?	*h*	did they?
d	will you?	*i*	will you?
e	aren't there?	*j*	aren't I?

Notes on pronunciation

You can change the meaning of a question tag by the way you say it. If your voice **falls** at the end of the question tag, you expect your listener to agree with you. It's not a real question. For example:

We've worked hard today, haven't we?

If your voice rises at the end, you sound questioning and you expect an answer (either 'yes' or 'no') from your listener. It **is** a real question. For example:

It's not time to go already, is it?

Practise saying the following sentences with both falling and rising intonation:

You can drive, can't you?
Your parents aren't coming, are they?
It's not 6 o'clock yet, is it?
She speaks Russian, doesn't she?
I don't have to pay, do I?

▶ Focus on writing 2 · Narrative (p. 147)

Note: This would be a suitable topic for a timed exam practice if you feel students would benefit from the experience of writing in a limited time at this stage of their course.

Read through the notes on the plan and on tenses. Check that students can say **why** the different tenses are used in the examples. In particular, revise the use of the past perfect to express the earlier of two actions in the past (examples *c* and *d*).

Find out how many students have had a personal 'narrow escape' that they can write about. Suggest that those who haven't should use the picture at the bottom of the page as the basis for an imaginary account.

If there are a number of students who will be writing an account based on the picture, it would be useful to give them time to work in a group (or groups) to discuss their ideas.

Make sure that all students make a brief plan before they start writing the composition.

▶ Exam practice A · Vocabulary (p. 148)

1	*c* (1.7, Unit 2A Study Box 2)	**14**	*a* (Lead-in 2e)
2	*d* (1.38)	**15**	*c* (Lead-in 2f)
3	*d* (Focus on grammar 1)	**16**	*d* (Focus on grammar 2)
4	*b* (2.21)	**17**	*d* (Study Box 2)
5	*c* (2.3)	**18**	*a* (Study Box 3)
6	*c* (1.32)	**19**	*b* (2.1, Study Box 3)
7	*a* (1.38)	**20**	*d* (Focus on grammar 1)
8	*b* (2.22)	**21**	*a* (Study Box 1)
9	*b* (Focus on grammar 2)	**22**	*c*
10	*b* (2.11)	**23**	*b* (Listening 1)
11	*a* (1.14)	**24**	*a* (Unit 4A, Focus on grammar 1)
12	*d* (Focus on grammar 3)	**25**	*b* (Unit 2B, Study Box 2)
13	*c* (Lead-in 2c)		

UNIT 5B The market place

▶ Lead-in · Topic vocabulary (p. 150)

The photograph can be used to provide practice for Paper 5 in the examination, the Interview.

Possible approaches

a Write a number of questions on the board. Students discuss the answers in pairs or small groups.

Example questions

What is the man selling?
Where do you think he gets these items from?
Who buys them?
What is the man with a hat holding in his hand?
Would you find a stall like this in your country? If so, where?
Would you be interested in looking at a stall like this? Why/why not?

b Students take it in turns to ask and answer questions about the picture.

c Students follow the 'Witness' procedure (see page 16).

d Perhaps initiate a brief discussion of different methods of buying and selling.

1 a a butcher   e a newsagent
   b a baker   f a tobacconist
   c a fishmonger   g a chemist/pharmacist
   d a greengrocer   h a grocer

2 a the box office   e a travel agent's (agency)
   b the booking office   f a stationer's
   c a bookshop   g an estate agent's
   d a petrol station/filling station/   h an ironmonger's
     service station/garage

3 a a hairdresser's (barber's)   c a laundry
   b a shoemender's/cobbler's   d a laundrette

4 a slice (cold meat*, cake**)   d roll (bandage, wallpaper)
   b bar (soap, chocolate)   e pair (sunglasses, gloves)
   c bunch (flowers, grapes)
     *although actually sold in slices, the cost is by weight
     **quite often also bought whole.

▶ Text 1 · Inside a supermarket (p. 151)

1 A basket   D till
   B check-out   E trolley
   C carrier bag   F bar-code

After students have discussed these questions, check their answers briefly, without confirming or denying anything.

The answers will become clear when students read the text. Don't forget to refer back to the questions at a later stage.

2 a 1912
   b USA
   c have to walk a long way to find what they want.

3 It is best if students work in pairs for this exercise, each looking at one set of questions.

Allow students time to read through their questions before they begin to look for answers in the text.

After students have finished exchanging information, check the answers by asking A students the answers to the B questions, and vice versa. This will check how well their partner explained, and how well they listened!

A 1 To encourage shoppers to use a trolly (instead of a basket).
   2 People are eating 30% more cereal and fewer cooked breakfasts.
   3 High-intensity lighting.
   4 The centres of freezer cabinets and the ends of aisles (because products sell very fast in those places).
   5 Bar-codes on packets which can be read by a special light pen will make it unnecessary to have individual price labels on products.

B 1 Because people tend to stop buying when their basket is full.
   2 Sugar.
   3 Tea, butter, pet food and soap.
   4 It was the first grocery with a check-out. It was a success and led to the opening of 2,800 other Piggly Wiggly stores.
   5 Because they lose 1 in 5 of their trolleys in a year.

Check answers to question 2 now.

Vocabulary included in Exam practice A: to pay for, to display/a display, receipt, to release, to replace, to add up, individual (adjective), in stock, a short cut.

▶ Focus on grammar 1 · The passive voice (p. 153)

Examples from the text

It *has been estimated* … The centres of free cabinets *are called* 'hot spots' … The purchase of some things … *is* usually *preplanned* … The bar-code … *will soon be used* … New trolleys … *are being tested* … £225 million *is spent* … Supermarkets *are laid out*.

Exercise 1 (Example answers)

Tense	Subject	Verb *to be*	Past participle
Present simple	Dinner	*is*	served.
Present continuous	A new hospital	is being	built.
Present Perfect	A stolen car	has been	found.
Past simple	The thief	was	*arrested*
Past continuous	The room	*was being*	painted.
Past Perfect	The decision	had been	taken.
Future simple	Your offer	will be	*considered*
Future perfect	*The invitations*	will have been	posted.
OTHER STRUCTURES			
Going to	His car	*is going to be*	serviced.
Modals (Present)	This machine	can *be*	mended.
(Past)	*This letter*	shouldn't have been	opened.

Exercise 2

1 g   5 f
2 c   6 b
3 h   7 d
4 a   8 e

Exercise 3 (Example answers)

a Dogs must/should be kept on a lead/under control.
b Cheques cannot be accepted./Payment cannot be made by cheque.
c Smoking is not allowed/permitted.
d Shoes must be removed (before entering the mosque).
e Cigarettes must/should be placed in the ashtrays.
f Helmets must/are to be worn on this site.

In each case, ask where the sign might be seen.

Exercise 4

a is cut down
b be built
c are spent
d also be saved; were made
e be ground up, mixed … and sold
f has only been beaten
g was probably painted
h was being washed
i is being written

j are still denied
k will not be forgotten
l have been delayed
m was split
n Will the votes be/have been counted
o had been broken into

▶ Focus on listening 1 · Chips with everything (p. 154)

System	Town	Equipment needed	Home delivery?	Cost
Over-60's Shopping Line	Gateshead	☎ ✓ / ▣ ✓ / ❓	✓	free
CLUB 403	Birmingham	☎ ✓ / ▣ ✓ / ❓	✓	£6.50 every 3 months
Shopping Link	South London	☎ ✓ / ▣ / ❓	✓	£1.73 for each order
Comp-u-Card	Windsor	☎ / ▣ / ❓ ✓	✓	£20 to join.

Key: ☎ = telephone   ▣ = television   ❓ = no information

Vocabulary included in Exam practice A: stock.

▶ Text 2 · Buying by post (p. 155)

1 *b* check that the newspaper … is up to date. (1)
  c keep details of the advertisement … advertiser's address … (5)
  g When you write off (and … return goods) always include your name and address. (3)
  h Make sure you keep cheque stubs or counterfoils. (7)
  i Keep a … note of the date it was sent. (4)

2 Multiple-choice
  a **B** ('fit in seconds')
  b **D** ('Order now while stocks last.')
  c **A** ('without pulling or stretching their delicate fibres')
  d **B** ('Do not confuse with inferior models.')
  e **D** ('your worries are over.')
  f **A,C** ('No home should be without one', 'Indispensable/A must in any first-aid box.')

Vocabulary included in Exam practice A: to write off (for), a receipt, proof, to stretch, confuse *with*, relief, protect *from*, stock(s).

▶ Focus on writing · Formal letter (p. 156)

Suggested preparation
1 Revise details of formal letter writing:
  Layout – sender's and recipient's addresses; date; beginning and ending (see the model on page 98 and/or page 222).
  Style – neither too formal nor too colloquial (see note on page 99).
2 Draw up a suitable plan on the board, with the help of the class.
  First paragraph: Explain why you are writing.
  Middle paragraph(s): Give full details (see list under 'If you have to complain').
  Last paragraph: Explain what you would like the recipient to do.
3 (Optional) Check who the letter should be addressed and sent to (the Advertising Manager of the newspaper, **not** the company concerned). You may, however, prefer to wait and see how carefully students have read the instructions. If some make the mistake of writing to the company, it will provide a useful

warning, because in the examination they would get no marks!

▶ Communication activity · Selling pets (p. 156)

Preparation
You may prefer to elicit selected items of functional language, put these on the board, and then practise for appropriate stress and intonation.

Decide which students should work together in pairs and ask them to read their instructions.

Find a way of telling A students which animal they have to sell without their partner hearing. The element of surprise created will help to make the role play more lively and realistic. You could either whisper the name of the animal or write it on slips of paper.

Once A students have told their partners which role to take, the role play should start.

Role play
Monitor the conversations but avoid offering advice or interrupting unless absolutely necessary. Note what language is used and what expressions are not included. Note, too, any particular errors.

After 5 minutes, tell students to change roles. Give B students the name of another animal in the way described above.

Feedback
Ask for brief responses from students to the discussion points. Deal with any language problems that you noted.

Note: Unless any pair particularly wants to perform their conversation in front of the class at this point, it is probably not a good idea to suggest it. The second-time-round conversations are likely to be more self-conscious and less spontaneous.

▶ Text 3 (p. 157)

Multiple-choice
  1 *c*
  2 *c* ('You are likely to spend less if you leave the children behind.')
  3 *a* ('Try to plan your cooking to have a full oven.')
  4 *b* ('Think particularly carefully about running a second car.')
  5 *d* ('Buying food in large packets and bulk quantities.')

Vocabulary included in Exam practice A: to get by (C), *take* advantage of (A).

▶ Focus on listening 2 · The auctioneer (p. 158)

Note: Before students open their books, introduce the topic by drawing an auctioneer's hammer on the board and asking what it is and where they would see it used. If the class needs more help, tell them it is associated with a particular kind of buying and selling.

Even if students don't know the term 'auction', ask them to describe how an auction works. Introduce the topic vocabulary from page 158 and ask if anyone has ever attended an auction.

How do you show that you want to bid? (Be careful not to give a definite right answer here.) What are the advantages and disadvantages? Are there any dangers?

Multiple-choice
  1 *c* ('an opportunity came up to move into the auction side of the business')
  2 *d* ('it's normally raising the catalogue')
  3 *c* ('it's often a bit of a joke; a bit of light relief')
  4 *a* ('getting slightly carried away')

True/false
  5 False. (a lot of people … want to go and have a look around the house as well as the contents)
  6 True. (in an appalling condition – you could hardly see what was actually underneath it)
  7 False. (we were hoping it would get something around there)

8 True.
9 False. (I'm called upon to value items in a very broad sense …)
10 furniture/wood
11 can't afford
12 scared

▶ Focus on grammar 2 · Gerund and infinitive (p. 159)

Exercise 1

a to call; to order
b typing; to concentrate
c to telephone; servicing
d to make; raining
e buying; painting; decorating
f to say; promising
g taking; to buy
h to try; shouting

Exercise 2

a asking; to raise; to do
b to stop; working; to call
c thinking; to lend
d using; to borrow; typing
e taking; not to call
f to hear; to visit; seeing

▶ Exam practice A · Vocabulary (p. 160)

1 a (3 C, (Unit 4A Study Box 2)
2 d (2,1)
3 b (2, Question 1)
4 b (1)
5 c (1)
6 b (2)
7 a (2)
8 b (2)
9 c (2)
10 c (1, 2, Listening 1)
11 c (2)
12 d (3 A)
13 d (1)
14 a (1)
15 c (1)
16 d (2)
17 b (1)
18 a (1)
19 a (Study Box 3)
20 b (Unit 5A, Study Box 2)
21 d (Unit 5A Study Box 3)
22 c (Unit 5A Study Box 1)
23 a (Unit 5A 1.6)
24 d (Unit 5A Focus on grammar 3)
25 c (Unit 5A Focus on grammar 1)

UNIT 6B Turning points

▶ Lead-in (p. 162)

Note: It is best if students work in pairs or small groups initially for this activity.

1 Ask students to decide what is happening (or has happened) in each picture, and to give reasons for their opinions, using information in the pictures. For example, 'In picture C, I think the couple have just got married because the woman is wearing a white dress and headdress, and is holding a bouquet of flowers.'

Remind students to use language which shows a range of probability. For example:

(I think) it/he/she/they	may could must	be	may could must	have been
he/she seems	+ adjective + to + infinitive			

Ask students to discuss the second part of question 1. For example:

A (first day at school): becoming more independent, making friends, developing interests in particular subjects which might lead to a career, etc.

2 Again ask students to discuss this question in pairs/groups and to try to reach agreement. They should be prepared to explain their reasons to the class afterwards.

3,4 These questions can be discussed by the class as a whole, unless numbers make this difficult.

▶ Lead-in 2 (p. 163)

Give students time to read through the extracts fairly quickly (2–3 minutes) and then ask them to discuss their ideas with another student.

Establish that they all refer to the experience of winning a large sum of money, and ask how this could have happened (football pools, lottery, etc).

1 a (possibly c)
2 c
3 They probably didn't feel that s/he was the same as them any more. They may have felt that it was strange to buy drinks for someone who was so much richer than they were, yet they didn't want him/her to pay for everything either.
4 He must have thought that he should have received some money, or else that his £800 wasn't a generous enough gift for his son.
5 Begging letters were letters from people asking for money. Proposals could have been offers of marriage, or perhaps offers concerning business matters. The winner's new friends must be people who are interested in her because of her new wealth. She's fed up with them because they aren't real friends, and they seem to be rather a nuisance.
6 A person might become proud/arrogant/snobbish. They might reject their old friends or show off to them by spending money in large amounts.
7 It depends on the friendship. I don't think it would affect a really old friendship which had lasted a number of years, but with newer friends, it could be difficult because suddenly my friend would be able to buy expensive things and take expensive holidays. The only way I could share my friend's new lifestyle would be if s/he paid for me, and that wouldn't be comfortable for either of us.

Vocabulary included in Exam practice A: to react (b), to give up (d) (see also Study Box 1).

▶Focus on grammar 1 · Expressing wishes and regrets (p. 163)

Exercise 1 (Example answers)

I wish/If only …

a it wasn't raining.
b I could drive./I knew how to drive.
c I didn't have such an awful headache./the party wasn't this evening.
d he/she didn't snore so loudly./I could get to sleep.
e there was/were more time.
f I had a map./knew the way.

Exercise 2 (Example answers)

I wish/If only …

a I hadn't been going so fast./I had had the brakes repaired.
b I had listened to the weather forecast./It hadn't started raining.
c I hadn't forgotten the cake./I had read the recipe more carefully.
d I hadn't been caught./I had kept away from crime.
e I had read the notice./I hadn't decided to sit down.
f I hadn't tried to cross this field./I had seen the bull in time.

Exercise 3 (Example answers)

a It's high time you cleaned it./had it cleaned!
b Suppose you had an accident./you had your luggage stolen.
c Why do you still treat me as if I were a child?
d She'd rather you took her fruit.

▶Text 1 · Just a normal day? (p. 165)

Pre-questions – suggested answers

1 She won it in a newspaper competition.
2 She suspected that she might have won on Saturday morning when she checked her competition card, but she was quite sure by 6 o'clock that evening.
3 She's afraid she won't be able to continue going to bingo with her friends.

Multiple-choice

4 c
5 b ('to save on electricity')
6 a ('You can't take it in, can you?')
7 c
8 d ('all my friends')

Discussion points B

1 a I would probably feel better if I took more exercise.
   b If she didn't have a dog for company, she'd be quite lonely.
   c If you won £1,000, how would you spend the money?
2,3 After students have decided individually on their answers to the three questions, monitor the pairwork. Note when and how accurately the second conditional is used and what reasons are given.

Ask pairs to report back. This will be more effective if students are asked to report back on what their **partner** said.

The sequel

Allow students to read these short texts silently and to comment on how accurate their predictions were (Discussion points A). Check comprehension as necessary.

Vocabulary included in Exam practice A: take something in (see also Study Box 2).

▶Focus on listening 2 · Is there life after redundancy? (p. 167)

1 Check the difference between 'to be made redundant' and 'to be dismissed' or 'to be sacked'.
2 Give students time to study the table before playing the tape.

		Previous career	Length of time (years)	Redundancy pay	New career	Where?	Success? Yes/No/ Too early to say
A	Brian Collins	1.Electrical Industry 2.Teaching Sailing	a. 4	b. £350	c. boat repair firm	Scotland	yes
B	William Rudd	Chemical company	d. 20	e. £70,000	butcher's shop	Central London	g. YES
C	Patricia and Rex Pole	h. bank	33	i. £30,000	j. running a pub	South coast	k. NO
D	Graham Clarke	l. Salesman	m. 27	n. £2,000	Magician	Colchester	o. Too early to say

▶Communication activity · Turning points in history (p. 167)

Note: Since few students are likely to know more than one or two answers for certain, it may be necessary to re-emphasise that they should guess those they don't know, and that they must choose an answer for each question.

1 Monitor students' discussions and be prepared to help with any vocabulary problems.

Check students' answers in a class discussion before they look up the answers on page 177. Ask those who are confident of an answer to give reasons.

2 Pairs could award themselves marks for correct answers so that there will be a winning pair in the general knowledge quiz.

3 For variety of interaction, ask pairs to form groups of four in order to discuss these two questions. Emphasise that they must agree on one answer in each case, and that they must be prepared to give their reasons. Ask groups to report back afterwards.

4 Again, this will be more effective, and involve more communication, if groups first 'brainstorm' their ideas. Each group can then make one or two suggestions for the class to consider.

Vocabulary included in Exam practice A: take place.

▶Focus on writing · Exam practice (p. 168)

The two Focus on writing sections in this unit provide practice in each of the main types of writing required in the examination: Speech, Discussion, Letter, Narrative and Description.

It is a good opportunity to review the main features of language, style and organisation in each case. In particular, stress the importance of planning the structure and content of a piece of writing, in note form, in advance. Lack of pre-planning is one of the most common reasons for poor work in the composition paper of the examination.

In general, it is a good idea to involve students in discussing how to tackle the various topics beforehand. Working in groups, they can read through the notes and refer to previous sections or to the Functions Bank, as indicated, before a whole-class summarising session. The final writing, however, should be done individually, and preferably within a time limit of 45 minutes per topic.

If students are shortly going to be taking the *First Certificate* examination, a timed practice session would be extremely useful. This should take 1½ hours and be under examination conditions (no discussion, no reference to Functions Banks or to dictionaries). Students should select **two** of the five topics given in Focus on writing 1 and 2, to be completed in the time.

Marks can be awarded according to the scale below, which is used by the examination board. Bear in mind, however, the need not to dishearten weak candidates too much at this stage.

18–20	Excellent	Natural English with minimal errors and complete realisation of the task set.
16–17	Very Good	Good vocabulary and structure, above the simple sentence level. Errors non-basic.
12–15	Good	Simple but accurate realisation of task. Sufficient naturalness, not many errors.
8–11	Pass	Reasonably correct if awkward *or* natural treatment of subject with some serious errors.
5–7	Weak	Vocabulary and grammar inadequate for the task set.
0–4	Very Poor	Incoherent. Errors showing lack of basic knowledge of English.

1 Speech

A useful preparation phase would be a 'brainstorming' session in groups of three–five. Students should be given about ten minutes to draw up a list of 15 items for possible inclusion in the list. This will help to stimulate ideas and provide practice in justifying choices. (Make it clear that they do not need to choose all (or any) of their personal eight items from the list they've drawn up in a group.)

2 Discussion

Again it is helpful if students work in groups to consider the three points under (*a*).

▶ Focus on grammar 2 · Conditional 3 (p. 169)

Exercise 1

a If Mrs Barrett hadn't bought the *Daily Mirror*, she wouldn't have taken part in the competition.
b If she had forgotten to check the numbers on her card, she wouldn't have won a million pounds.
c She wouldn't have rung her daughter if she hadn't been so excited.
d If Annie hadn't been so tired, she wouldn't have gone back to sleep.
e She wouldn't have been interviewed if she hadn't become a millionairess.
f (Example answer) If she hadn't won so much money, she couldn't have moved from her council flat or bought a new television.

Exercise 2

a If the Incas had had paper, their architects wouldn't have needed to make clay models for the builders to follow./their architects could have drawn plans for the builders to follow.
b If Napoleon hadn't died in 1821, he might have had his photograph taken./If the camera had been invented earlier, Napoleon might have been photographed.
c Many lives would have been lost during World War II if penicillin hadn't been invented.
d Christopher Columbus might not have reached the West Indies in 1492 if the mariner's compass hadn't been invented.
e (Example answer) If tobacco hadn't been imported to Europe in 1553, the habit of smoking might never have developed.

Exercise 3

a If the Suez Canal hadn't been opened in 1869, ships would have to travel round Africa to reach India.
b If the Panama Canal hadn't been completed in 1914, ships would have to sail round South America to reach the Pacific.
c Ships would have to go round the Peloponnese to reach the Aegean Sea if the Corinth Canal hadn't been built in 1893.

Optional extra practice

Work with a partner. Think what life would be like today if the things below had never been invented. Discuss how your lives would be different.

a Clock (1290)
b Wheel (4,000 BC)
c Telephone (1876)
d Television (1926)

▶ Text 2 · What made David Cassidy retire at 25? (p. 170)

Ask if any of the students have heard of David Cassidy. (It's possible some of the older ones might have!) If not, don't reveal the answer to the question in the title yet, but ask students to guess from the clues in the photographs.

Ask students to suggest what might make a very successful pop star decide to retire at an early age.

Pre-questions – example answers

1 He was a pop singer with millions of fans.
2 He had a frightening experience at a concert in New York which made him realise that he wasn't enjoying his life at all and that he would have to give up his career if he wanted a normal life.
3 He stopped singing and travelled the world, seeing the things he'd missed before.

4 Vocabulary matching

a triumph (10)	f it hit me (37)
b hysterical (22)	g digested (44)
c rumble (24)	h handful (59)
d dumped (30)	i adulation (61)
e dive (33)	

Multiple-choice

1 c ('The entire building seemed to rumble ...')
2 c ('I was having no fun at all')
3 d
4 b
5 a ('I was just lucky ... I could have been on the casualty list')

(Optional questions on Footnote)

a What was the second turning point in David's life?
b What are some of his friends afraid of?
c Does the writer share his friend's opinion? Why/Why not?

Vocabulary included in Exam practice A: end *in* (14), audience (17), used to + *gerund* (21/22), arrange *for* (29), wrap (29), afford (49), *either ... or* (55).

▶ Focus on grammar 3 · Review of tenses (p. 172)

1 a I'll give; he comes in.
b He ran; he got; the bus had already gone.
c I wouldn't offer; I thought; wouldn't pay.
d You've broken; you'll have to
e does this train get
f It says; paintings have been stolen.
g I told; I wanted; I had found.
h you don't/won't stop; I'll call.
i We're going; it will be; we usually tour
j you haven't been waiting; the lift has broken down; I had to.
k we were waiting; the pilot announced; we were going to fly/would be flying
l I've been working; this page is finished; I'll have written.
m We bought; we needn't have done so.

n I hadn't seen; I would never have believed.

o you didn't smoke; you don't mind; smoke always makes.

2 *A* I haven't seen; have you been doing?

  B I've been working; I had; I only got.

  A were you living?

  B I spent; I went.

  A did you manage

  B I climbed; I also saw; it is called.

  A did you take

  B didn't come out; I was using; didn't have; I had taken

  A you'll show; I had known you were going; I would have asked.

  B I was invited; I didn't have

  A I was only joking; are you doing

  B My parents are coming; they will leave/will have left.

  A don't you come; you'll be able to

  B I'll even bring

3

Paragraph 1	*Paragraph 2*
left	decided
to get round	to take
must have written	to earn
said	to pay
to tell	was serving
applied	talking
has now been filled	explained/was explaining
had	had left/was leaving
told	didn't know
had been	to do
didn't get	stopped
	serving
	asked
	would consider
	had
	must have been
	agreed
	to interview
	was given
	am working
	would still be serving
	hadn't had

▶ Focus on listening 2 · A new direction (p. 173)

Find out if students remember the conversation with John, the merchant seaman, from Unit 2A. For example, ask questions like:

How long did he work in the Merchant Navy?
Did he enjoy the life?
Why did he leave?

Point out that the conversation they are going to hear is with the same man, and in it he discusses the complete change of career which occurred after he left the Merchant Navy.

True/false

1 False. ('I remembered seeing the nurses work in hospital and I thought "I'd quite like to do that" ')

2 False. ('I could've worked in a hotel ...')

3 True. ('... provided you have the right educational qualifications')

4 False. ('I started where I finished ... I never left it.')

5 True. ('... 3 years' training initially and then ... 2 years' training in mental illness')

6 False. ('There's really no difference.')

7 True.

8 True. ('The pay was very low compared with the Merchant Navy')

9 True. (Most were in their teens. He was 31.)

10 False. ('I didn't want to be living in the nurses' home ...')

11 *b* ('moving from ward to ward')

12 *c* (I wanted to go on learning ... it was the next logical step.)

13 *d* ('No regrets whatsoever. Even the bad things I don't regret.')

▶ Focus on writing 2 · Exam practice (p. 174)

For general notes about the writing tasks in this unit, see Focus on writing 1 (page 168).

1 Letter

The main points to revise here are the *layout* of a personal letter and aspects of language and style (see pages 28/29 and 220/221).

A good way of revising these would be to produce a 'bad' letter which includes examples of all the common mistakes (for example, 'Dear Friend', no paragraphs, wrong use of 'Yours faithfully', etc.) and ask students in pairs to identify the faults. Alternatively, elicit the main points from the students.

2 Narrative

Revise expressions of time and the use of the past tenses, as indicated. Refer students to the paragraph plan on page 147 and Writing Bank pages 229/230.

3 Description

Pictures from magazines can be used to revise the language of physical description and also aspects of character and mood. For example:

S/he looks | rather | serious/threatening/nervous/shy.
        | very | friendly/cheerful/sociable/confident.

See Functions Bank page 214 and Writing Bank pages 225/226.

▶ Exam practice A · Vocabulary (p. 175)

1 *d* (2.29)	16 *a*
2 *c* (Lead-in 2b)	17 *d* (Unit 1B Focus on grammar 1)
3 *c* (2.21/22)	
4 *c* (2.55)	18 *a* (Unit 2A Listening 2)
5 *d* (2.29)	19 *b* (Unit 2A Focus on grammar 1)
6 *b* (2.49)	
7 *b* (1.90, Study Box 2)	20 *d* (Functions Bank, Expressing Opinions)
8 *a* (2.14)	
9 *c* (2.17)	21 *b* (Unit 2B Focus on grammar 1)
10 *d* (Communication activity)	
11 *c* (Focus on grammar 2)	22 *b* (Unit 3A Study Box 1)
12 *a* (Writing 1)	23 *c* (Lead-in 2d, Study Focus on Box 1)
13 *b* (Unit 6A Focus on grammar 3)	
	24 *d* (Unit 2B Study Box 1)
14 *c* (Unit 6A Study Box 1)	25 *a* (Unit 3B Study Box 1)
15 *b* (Focus on grammar 1)	

EXAM PRACTICE B

▶ **Use of English · Units 1A/1B** (p. 178)

1 *a*
1	which/that	11	had
2	across/over	12	to
3	in	13	but
4	in	14	before
5	go	15	As/since/because
6	happens	16	been
7	that	17	before/earlier
8	will	18	took
9	on	19	to
10	has	20	read/study/examine

1 *b*
1	for	11	are
2	before	12	the
3	out	13	from/and
4	which/that	14	from
5	exist	15	where
6	regions/areas/ice	16	on
7	peaks/heights/mountains	17	can/may/might/will
8	them	18	from/at
9	in	19	Others/some
10	in	20	climbing

2 *a* He's very keen on playing football.
 b The cost of travelling by coach/coach travel is going to go up/ rise/increase (is going up/rising/increasing) next year.
 c In spite of the heavy rain, we all …
 d There used to be a shop near here which/that sold …
 e When we arrived (at 6 o'clock) the train had just/already left.
 f It's worth taking/remembering to take …
 g It was such an unexpected remark that …
 h That's the woman whose dog bit …
 i There was some difficulty in persuading her …
 j A saw is a tool for cutting/that you use for cutting/that is used for cutting …

3 *a* trips/excursions *d* voyage
 b cruise *e* travel
 c flight

4 *a* complaint *f* receipt
 b absence *g* harmless
 c response *h* heightened
 d relief *i* solution
 e representative *j* disembarked

5 *a* I am writing to complain about a/the holiday which/that was arranged by your company.
 b My wife and I booked a two-week cruise on the "Orient Maiden" in July this year.
 c The brochure described it as the holiday of a lifetime so we decided to spend all our savings on it.
 d We expected a luxury ship with first class service but the cabins were dirty and the waiters (were) rude.
 e The ship was supposed to call at Naples and Athens but the captain said it was/would be impossible because of the bad weather.
 f There was nothing at all to do on the ship except (to) watch (the) old films in the cinema.
 g We were seriously dissatisfied with the cruise and (we) want our money back.

h If we don't hear from you in the next seven days, we will contact our solicitor.

▶ **Use of English · Units 2A/2B** (p. 181)

1 *a*
1	at	11	had
2	have	12	took/passed
3	The/an	13	became
4	grew	14	do/take/follow
5	at	15	lasted/took
6	study/read	16	At/by
7	going	17	was
8	missed/lacked/wanted	18	made
9	would	19	as
10	But	20	own

1 *b*
1	grow/produce	11	growing
2	feed	12	see/know/recognise
3	they	13	make/take
4	for	14	one/person
5	few	15	in
6	situation/position	16	comforts/helps
7	Unless	17	by
8	no/little	18	doing
9	away/far	19	too
10	manages/tries	20	land/crops

2 *a* The water was too cold (for me) to swim in. (Not 'in it'.)
 b I'd rather travel by train than go by air.
 c His secretary told me that he had gone home five minutes earlier/before and had taken his papers with him.
 d The more carefully you work, the fewer mistakes you ('ll) make.
 e You're the worst driver in the world.
 f The waiter warned me not to touch the plate because it was hot.
 g Our car is big enough to take/for five passengers.
 h He apologised for keeping me waiting.
 i The bus often takes longer/more time than the underground.

3 *a* put the meeting *off* (postpone)
 b put you *through* (connect)
 c put him *up* (give him a bed)
 d put *on* (gained)
 e put me *off* (discouraged)
 Reference: Unit 2A, Study Box 3 (p. 27).

4 *a* relationship *f* noisily
 b monthly (month's) *g* distinction
 c endless *h* removal
 d offence *i* unreliable
 e librarian *j* helpful

5 *a* I am writing to tell you that I am rather worried about your son Peter who is a pupil in my class.
 b Peter has been absent from school on several occasions in/ during the last three weeks.
 c He did not give any reason for his absence and (he) refused to apologise. (has not given … has refused …)
 d He is an intelligent boy and has always been near the top of the class up till now.
 e Unfortunately his work is now beginning to suffer and his marks are very poor. (has now begun … have been …)
 f Unless there is a big improvement in his attendance and work, he is unlikely to pass his 'O' Levels.
 g I think it would be a good idea if we could meet/met to discuss the/this problem.
 h I would be grateful if you could telephone me at school to arrange an appointment to see me.

▶ **Use of English · Units 3A/3B** (p. 184)

1 *a*
1 up
2 between
3 than
4 from
5 It
6 met
7 told
8 being
9 as
10 had/took/started
11 for/about
12 at/during
13 in
14 By
15 least
16 take
17 wake/get
18 only
19 who
20 both

1 *b*
1 do/manage
2 as
3 on
4 wheel
5 with
6 at
7 for
8 are
9 from
10 nothing/little
11 that/which
12 well
13 save
14 seriously
15 call/see/visit/consult
16 At
17 it
18 at
19 obtained/given
20 All/what

2 *a* It's the first time (that) she's been to a circus.
  b He asked the guard how long the journey would take.
  c Since the accident he hasn't been able to work.
  d There were twice as many guests as they (had) expected.
  e Neither of my brothers is married.
  f That's the cat whose owner feeds it on …
  g He said 'How about going to the theatre?'
  h How long have you had a broken arm? (… has your arm been broken?)
  i A great deal of money was given to the Earthquake Disaster Fund.

3 *a* get *on with* (manage to work/live with)
  b *getting* me *down* (causing depression)
  c get *round to* (find time for)
  d get *by* (survive/manage to live)
  e get it *back* (regain possession)
  f get *out of* (avoid doing)
References: Units 4A, Study Box 2 (p. 52) and 2B, Study Box 2 (p. 113).

4 *a* over*board*
  b neighbour*hood*
  c loud*speaker*
  d land*lord*
  e broad*cast*
  f head*quarters*
  g shop*keeper*
  h back*ground*
  i out*look*
  j head*long*

5 *a* Why do you need it?/Why do you want to borrow it?
  b How long have you been interested in (photographing) wild birds?
  c Are you sure you know how to use it?/You don't know how to use it, do you?
  d Well, only if you promise to take very good care of it./… to look after it very carefully./… to take great care when you're using it.
  e All right. But you'll have to buy your own film for it. You can't have any of mine!

▶ **Use of English · Units 4A/4B** (p. 187)

1 *a*
1 to
2 place
3 make
4 fetch/collect
5 these/those/such
6 happen/occur
7 left
8 drove
9 sure
10 worth
11 in
12 off
13 step
14 into
15 be
16 could/might/would
17 has
18 seeing/finding
19 least
20 loss(es)

1 *b*
1 make/take
2 sitting
3 to
4 with
5 which/that
6 As/while
7 feel/get
8 shot/fired
9 had
10 able
11 earth/land
12 was
13 said/explained/commented
14 hit/touch
15 be/get
16 for
17 broke
18 soon
19 will
20 had

2 *a* We've got to get to the airport …
  b The robber may/might/could have hidden his gun …
  c It's no use crying.
  d You needn't/don't need to/don't have to make an appointment.
  e Having thrown away the receipt, I couldn't …
  f It wasn't until I got your card that I remembered …
  g There were steep hills on either/each side of the road. (on both sides of the road)
  h I'll look for a new coat as soon as the sale starts.
  i He folded the letter so as to get it through …

3 *a* broke *out* (escaped)
  b break *off* (end suddenly)
  c broke *down* (collapsed)
  d broken *in* (entered by force)
  e break *down* (fail to go on working)
  f broken *up* with (separated from)
  g break *in* (interrupt)
Reference: Unit 4A, Study Box 3 (p. 54).

4 *a* Look *out!* (take care)
  b looking *into* (investigating)
  c look *up* (search for information)
  d look *after* (take care of)
  e look *in* (visit)
  f looked *up* to (respected)
  g looking *for* (trying to find)
  h I looked *through* (examined)
Reference: Unit 2B, Study Box 1 (p. 106).

5 *a* Oh yes, sir. Where was it stolen from?
  b Do you know when it was taken?
  c Can you describe the car?/What does the car look like?
  d And was there anything valuable inside the car?
  e You ought to have taken those with you, or at least locked them in the boot.

▶ **Use of English · Units 5A/5B** (p. 190)

1 *a*
1 on
2 the
3 coast/shores
4 up
5 By
6 had
7 least
8 In
9 Before
10 proportion/amount/part
11 carrying
12 would
13 there
14 amounts/quantities
15 can/may
16 instance/example
17 for
18 less
19 spoil/ruin/destroy
20 from

1 *b*
1 than
2 at
3 over/above
4 A/Your
5 By
6 have
7 keeping
8 during/for
9 off
10 yourself
11 or
12 need/have
13 of
14 of
15 costs
16 for
17 while
18 doing
19 go
20 ways

2 *a* Unless someone mends the roof, it will collapse.
  b Smoking is not only expensive but (it is) also harmful to the

health.

c I'm looking forward to having a holiday (soon)/(... to my holiday).

d Several trees were blown down by the wind.

e 'I wonder if I could/might use your phone?'

f There was a delay as a result of a signal box failure.

g If I were you, I'd take my/your/the dog ...

h My mother prefers playing cards to knitting.

i Have you had your cooker mended?

3 a went *through* (searched)

b going *down with* (becoming ill)

c goes *in for* (enters)

d gone *off* (exploded)

e goes *with* (matches)

Reference: Unit 4B, Study Box 1 (p. 136).

4 a contents   f convenience

b discouraged   g variety

c destruction   h Sales

d discovery   i growth

e accidentally

5 1 Do you know what size you take/want?

2 What material would you like/were you thinking of?

3 That will be quite expensive/cost quite a lot.

4 How do you like this one?

5 Why not try it on?

6 Does it fit (you)/feel comfortable?

7 Here's one in a larger/bigger size.

8 Would you like me to wrap it up?

▶ Use of English · Units 6A/6B (p. 193)

1 a

1 had	11 from
2 was	12 Instead
3 in	13 by
4 who	14 in
5 calls	15 dumb
6 name	16 sense
7 used/designed/able	17 getting/moving/turning/going
8 At	18 own
9 over	19 in
10 in	20 with

1 b

1 met/saw/passed	11 as
2 a	12 like
3 what	13 out
4 on	14 won
5 which	15 by
6 less	16 directories/books
7 given	17 on/up
8 spend/use	18 were
9 us/you	19 range/series
10 kind/sort/type	20 about

2 a I haven't played tennis for ten years.

b I'll give you a lift, if you like.

c He'd rather you didn't buy him anything expensive.

d If you had been listening you would have understood.

e If only I hadn't left home when I was 18.

f She used to sing better than she does now.

g By 1.15 I'll have had/eaten lunch.

h In case I'm not in when you get home, I'll give you ...

i Do you mind telling me what you're doing in my room?

3 a takes *after* (resembles)

b took *up* (adopted as a pastime)

c taken *on* (accepted)

d take you *in* (deceive)

e take *over* (assume control)

Reference: Unit 6B, Study Box 1 (p. 171).

4 a make   f making

b did   g done

c made   h made

d do   i Make

e done   j doing

Reference: Unit 2A, Study Box 2 (p. 23)

5 a I was delighted to receive your letter which arrived this morning.

b It has been so long since we last met that I was sure you had forgotten me.

c I can hardly believe (that) you have been married for six years and (that you) have two children.

d If you have any photographs of the/your family, I would love to see them.

e I am still single but the good news is that I am getting (am going to get) married in February.

f It would be wonderful if you could come to the/my wedding.

g I'll send (you) an invitation as soon as I/we know the date and (the) place.

h I look forward to hearing from you again.

EXAM PRACTICE C

The six oral packages in this section are linked to topics in the book and can either be introduced gradually, one every two units, or reserved for intensive practice when students have completed the twelve units.

The packages may be used for guided examination preparation, or as practice tests under examination conditions.

▶ Examination procedure

1 Group or individual?

It is now possible for examination centres to choose between individual and group interviews, as mentioned in the Introduction. The advantage of the group option is that it allows for more natural and realistic communication of a kind that will be extremely familiar to students who have participated in the communicative activities in this book.

Note: If your local centre is unable, for practical reasons, to offer the group option, there are still a number of advantages in conducting some of the practice tests in groups:
– students will co-operate, learning from each other's strengths.
– more communication will be generated.
– the experience will be less isolating and more confidence-building.

2 Optional reading

Candidates may choose to discuss one of three set texts as the basis for Section C in the Interview. Since these texts vary from year to year, it is not possible to include example questions in this practice material. An up-to-date list of set texts is included in the current Regulations published by the University of Cambridge Local Examinations Syndicate.

3 Interview sections

Section 1: Picture conversation (about 6 minutes)

The examiner asks questions about a photograph and leads on to more general discussion of related themes. In a group interview, candidates may also be required to ask questions themselves.

Section 2: Reading passages (about 3 minutes)

Two short passages are used as the basis for a discussion between the examiner and the candidate, or between candidates. Reading aloud is no longer required, although candidates may quote from the texts to illustrate their comments.

Section 3: Structured communication activity (about 6 minutes)

A wide range of activities based on pictures, diagrams or texts is used. These may include advertisements, timetables, weather reports, questionnaires, maps, etc. Candidates may be required to take part in a role play, solve a problem or discuss opinions. They may also choose to discuss a set book during this section.

4 Marking

The three sections of the Interview are assessed **as a whole** on six scales, each of 0–5 marks. The scales are as follows:

Fluency
Grammatical accuracy
Pronunciation: prosodic features (stress, rhythm, etc.)
Pronunciation: individual sounds
Communicative ability
Vocabulary

A broadly adequate mark, as suggested by the Cambridge Syndicate, is 60% or 18 out of 30.

Note: Marks scored in Paper 4 (Listening Comprehension) and Paper 5 (Interview) together now account for one-third of the total marks in the examination.

▶ Examination preparation

Section 1: Picture conversation

It is important to point out to students that the picture itself merely serves as a jumping-off point for conversation. The Interview is not a test of general knowledge but of the language skills listed in the previous section.

If it is not clear what is shown in a picture, or if a question is difficult to answer, it is perfectly valid to say so! What matters is to give the examiner sufficient opportunity to assess a candidate's English. This means giving full answers and illustrating remarks with examples where appropriate.

In particular, remind students of the language of speculation for expressing degrees of certainty (see page 23 in this book).

If students will be having the Interview in a group, they should also be given the opportunity to practise asking each other questions about these and other pictures.

Recommended procedures

'Witness' (see page 52 in the Student's Book).

Groupwork: students working together to answer the questions given, pooling ideas and vocabulary.

'Mock' interviews: students in pairs, one acting as 'examiner'.

'Mock' interviews: teacher and student(s).

Section 2: Reading passages

Again point out to students that this is not a test of reading comprehension. It is the way that they express their reactions to the passages, in English, that will be assessed. Reassure them that they will be given enough time to read through the passages and that, if there is a word or phrase they really don't understand, they should feel free to say so.

The candidates will normally be asked:

– What the passage is about, or if there is a common theme between two passages.
– Where the passage(s) might have come from, and whether they were originally written or spoken.
– Who the speaker or writer might have been, and what their intention was.

Students need to be trained to look for clues in the texts which give an indication as to the source and the writer's intention. They also need to be able to recognise differences of style between spoken and written English (see page 36 in the Student's Book).

Encourage students to illustrate their comments by giving short quotations from the texts (i.e. words or phrases rather than whole sentences).

Recommended procedures

Students read passages individually and then discuss their ideas about them with a partner. After that, **either** pairs team up to form groups of four, and then compare their conclusions; **or** pairs split up and new pairs are formed for further discussion.

'Mock' interviews: students read passages individually and then discuss their reactions individually or in groups with the teacher.

Note: If the students are weak in this aspect of the examination, it is helpful if the teacher designs focus questions for the first one or two practice sessions. These can be simple gist comprehension questions, or they can draw students' attention to key features in the passages.

Section 3: Structured communication activity

Of the six activities included, three involve co-operation between students (1, 3, 4), and three involve a role playing element (2, 5, 6).

Point out how important it is to read the instructions carefully before beginning. After that, a pair or group should check that everyone understands exactly what to do. If they need to discuss how to tackle a particular task, how to start, or who should take which part, that will generate perfectly valid communication. The language produced in *talking about* the activity is just as useful to the examiner in assessing candidates as the language used in *participating in* the activity.

For this reason, it's best to keep explanations to a minimum and to let students have practice in using the kind of transactional language needed to work things out. For example:

How shall we start?
Why don't you take the part of ... ?
Who's going to write the answers down?
Shall we move our chairs?

Recommended procedures

Students work in groups on a task simultaneously.

Half the class is divided into groups to work on a task while the others act as observers, taking notes on what they hear and reporting back to the groups later.

One group works on a task while the rest of the class observes and makes notes. The 'performance' is then discussed by the class in relation to the scales used by the examiners. This provides useful reminders to students, particularly those who speak too much or too little!

Note: The last two approaches help to prepare students for the inevitable examination nerves and get them used to working together under observation.

'Mock' interview: one group works on a task under the observation of the teacher.

▶ Interview No 1 (Topic: work) (p. 196)

Section 1

Window-cleaners at work on a high-rise building.

Section 2

 a Advice on attending an interview, probably aimed at young people. Written English – from a magazine article, leaflet or book.
 b A personal account of a first job (in fact, given by Freddie Laker, who went on to establish his own airline in the 1970s). Written or spoken English.

Section 3

This is a fairly straightforward discussion topic for two or three students. It may help to make the conversation more purposeful if groups are told they will have to report back to the class or to another group.

▶ Interview No 2 (Topic: family Life) (p. 198)

Section 1

An elderly woman (grandmother?) with a young child, probably in a southern European country.

Section 2

 a A personal account of family life, probably in a Third World country, which could have been spoken or written. Obviously it is likely to have been translated from the original language. (In fact, it was taken from an account given by Bibi, a 12-year-old Bangladeshi girl.)
 b Part of an article from a daily newspaper describing the effects on the family life of an Indian family that immigration to Britain has had.

Section 3

Role play. There are three roles: A – child, B – parent; C – grandparent. Let students decide who is to be A, B and C, read through the notes for their roles and study the report on page 199. They should then make sure they know who the other members of the group represent. It's helpful if A and B are given names.

Give students a chance to ask questions before they begin the role play.

▶ Interview No 3 (Topic: health) (p. 200)

Section 1

Children's exercise or dance class.

Section 2

 a An explanation of stress – it is most likely to be written English from a magazine article or health leaflet, but could also have been part of a radio programme.
 b A description of the effect colours can have on feelings. It is probably spoken English (because of the opening questions) from a radio programme or talk.

Section 3

This is another fairly straightforward discussion topic, as in Interview 1. It requires the expression of opinions and the negotiation of answers in the pair or group.

Appropriate expression within the group discussion is what is important rather than knowing what the 'right' answers are.

Be prepared to help students with unfamiliar vocabulary, if necessary (for example, *liver, kidney, fatty, sardines, mackerel, kippers, helping, wholegrain*).

▶ Interview No 4 (Topic: safety) (p. 202)

Section 1

Firemen at the scene of a burning car.

Section 2

 a Advice on dealing with fireworks. This is written English, perhaps on the box of fireworks itself or in a safety leaflet.
 b Advice on dealing with a fire in a (chip) pan in the kitchen. This is spoken English (because of the last question) – probably a cookery teacher or a lecturer on fire safety.

Section 3

This is a co-operative problem-solving task. The eleven dangers are:

1 Toy left behind electric kettle, encouraging a child to reach for it and pull the kettle over.
2 Electric kettle flex stretching over the cooker.
3 Tea towels drying over the cooker.
4 Saucepan handle sticking out where a child might try to take hold of it.
5 Iron left on the ironing board.
6 Iron plugged into the electric light socket.
7 Cigarette left burning in an ashtray near newspaper.
8 Overloaded socket on the wall to the right of the door.
9 Matches left lying around for a child to experiment with.
10 Sharp knife left within reach of a child.
11 Cleaning materials, including bleach, left within reach of child.

Note: Students may not know the exact words for all the safety hazards but should try to use the vocabulary they have to express what they want to.

Students may also not be able to find all eleven safety hazards, but should stop after five minutes and move on to the second part of the task, the list of instructions.

▶Interview No 5 (Topic: buying and selling) (p. 204)

Section 1

Street market scene (rugs and carpets). The man is showing a rug to an interested couple.

Section 2

a Advertisement for a dishwashing machine. It was originally written, but could also have been spoken.

b Car salesman talking to a woman customer.

Section 3

Role play. There are three roles: A: shopkeeper; B: conservationist; C: developer. Let students decide who is to be A, B and C, read through their roles and study the information and map on page 205. Then give them the chance to ask questions.

▶Interview No 6 (Topic: animals and people) (p. 206)

Section 1

An old man with his faithful dog; a young boy with his pet budgerigar perched on his finger.

Section 2

a A vet speaking or writing about a dog's behavioural problems.

b A TV producer speaking or writing about his/her experiences working with donkeys in a television studio.

Section 3

Role play. The instructions are largely self-explanatory. Let students decide who is to be A, B and C, read through the notes and study the map. Then give them the opportunity to ask questions.

TAPESCRIPTS

UNIT 1A

▶ **Focus on listening 1** (p. 9)

A = Travel agent   B = Client

A Good morning. Can I help you?

B Yes, I wonder if you can give me some information about Crete as a place to go on holiday?

A Of course, what would you like to know?

B Well, I've looked through several brochures and I've picked out four hotels which are about the same price and which sound quite nice. But there's not a lot of information in the brochure and I wondered if you could tell me anything more, because I don't want to end up in a hotel near a discotheque, or where you have to walk five miles to the beach either!

A Right. Well, we have a gazetteer that'll be able to tell us that.

B A what?

A A gazetteer. It's a book which lists all the hotels and describes them, you know. It's supposed to tell the truth. Let me just go and get it!

B Oh, great.

A Now, which hotels were you interested in?

B Let me see, the first one's called the Concord.

A The Concord, right.

B I wondered what sort of building – is it an old style or what?

A Yes, here it is – the Concord. Let's see what it says – a pleasant three-storey building – so it's probably an older type of building, yes. It's about five minutes walk from the centre of town and a little less from the harbour. Quite a good situation.

B Does it say if it's near the beach?

A Yes. It says it has a terrace at the rear which leads directly on to a beach of sand and rock.

B So I wouldn't have to cross a road to get to the beach?

A No, it leads directly on to the beach, so there's no problem.

B That's fine then. Another one was called the Royal.

A The Royal. Right, yes.

B Yes, that one said that there was a discotheque nearby. I was quite worried about that.

A Right. Let's see what this one says. Yes. It's a three-storey building again, but a modern one. It says it has a curved front. It's also got a good-sized swimming pool and a discotheque situated well away from the bedrooms. So you're not going to be disturbed at night too much.

B Does it say where it is?

A Yes. On a cliff top with steps leading down to a pebble beach. Good bus service to the town centre – so it's obviously a bit out of town.

B Steps down to the beach – well, they should keep me fit, I suppose. Fine. Alright. Let's try another one. The Atlantic.

A The Atlantic – strange name for Crete!

B Yes. That one said it was on a main road. That could be noisy, couldn't it?

A Definitely. Right. It's described as a brightly decorated, simple hotel, one of a number recently built alongside the busy main road. There's a picture of it here – look. There are some trees in the front garden which would help to screen it from the road but I'm afraid you're bound to get some traffic noise. It says there's a poor beach opposite but a better one ten minutes' away. So …

B Well, ten minutes doesn't sound too bad but I don't like the idea of traffic noise. The last one I wanted to ask you about is called the Plaza.

A Right. That's described as a long low building standing high above the main road with an entrance up a steep slope. It's obviously not suitable for elderly or disabled people then. All rooms have balconies and excellent views over the bay. Just a few houses and villas nearby. Hotel transport to the beach.

B That sounds alright. And … did it say every room had a balcony?

A All rooms have balconies.

B Oh, marvellous! But do you think it would be noisy?

A Well, it says standing high above the main road. So, no I don't think noise would be too much of a problem.

B That's fine then. Now would you be able to give me the price of a flight only?

A Yes, certainly. Let me just get one or two of our flight-only brochures. Right. They have various flights on Fridays and Tuesdays. Now, when do you want to go?

B About the third week in July.

A About the third week. So we're looking at the twenty-first. Tends to be one of the most expensive times to go because that's when the schools break up. Anyway, they go … they range from £159, all the way up to £191. And that really depends on the flight times.

B OK. And is it advisable to have travel insurance?

A Definitely.

B How much would that cost?

A Roughly … Well, I can get a leaflet. Hold on. Well, this one … covers you very very well. It's the most comprehensive policy. And up to two weeks – it's £14.25. This other one we use mainly for students and it doesn't actually cover for cash loss. It's a bit cheaper, though, and that's £10.80.

B Well, thank you very much. That's very helpful. Can I think about it and perhaps call in tomorrow morning?

A Yes. No problem. We're open from 9 till 4 so just pop in any time and we'll see what we can do.

B Right. Thanks very much. Bye.

A OK. Thanks. Bye bye.

▶ **Focus on listening 2** (p. 11)

A = Continuity announcer   B = Presenter

A … And now we come to the programme which gives advice to consumers, *Your Buy*, and here's Mary Simmonds to introduce today's edition.

B Hello, well with the holiday season approaching, we thought it would be a good time to have a look at the subject of suitcases. There are a few people, I know, who use the same old suitcase all their lives. It may be a fine old leather one, covered with labels and stickers from the exotic places they've visited, for example.

Most suitcases, though, don't have quite such a long life and they need to be replaced from time to time. Leather is a bit too expensive to consider these days and it does tend to be rather heavy, too, and for those of us who are looking for something more practical, modern suitcases have a lot of advantages to offer.

In the first place, modern materials like nylon or vinyl can be both extremely tough and yet light enough to carry easily. There are basically two sorts of suitcase – soft ones, made from nylon, vinyl or PVC, and rigid ones, made from materials like ABS or polypropylene.

The second advantage modern suitcases have is that they often offer greater security than the old-fashioned kind. Most have locks or lockable catches of some kind, some have padlocks, and a few even have combination locks to outwit even the most determined thief.

Lastly, most up-to-date suitcases are made with wheels attached so that they can be pulled or pushed instead of carried. Again, there are two main types. Four-wheeled suitcases are designed to be pulled along, parallel to the floor. Suitcases with two wheels are tipped on one end and then either pulled or pushed, using a strap or handle on one side of the case. The four-wheeled sort are more likely to get damaged.

We've chosen four different suitcases to tell you about today. They range in price from the very cheap to the exclusive and expensive!

The first is the Riviera, which is in the middle price bracket. It's 67cm in length, in smart black PVC with contrasting grey trim. It has four wheels and a towing strap and it was very easy to manoeuvre when we tested it. It's fastened with a medium weight nylon zip, which has a two-year guarantee, and it also has a padlock which gives greater security. It costs £67 and we think it represents good value for money.

The second case, the Windsor, is the cheapest at £32.50 and it's widely available from chain stores all round the country. It's 68cm long and made of nylon in a choice of three colours and brown trim. There are two wheels and a strap on one side for pushing or pulling it along. It has five separate catches to fasten it and two of these are lockable. All in all it seems good value but the material is not very strong and we thought it might easily get torn.

Our third case is the Tornado and this is made of very tough ABS material in a plain cream colour. It's 75cm long and has two combination locks, which makes it the most secure of all the cases we tested. If you have a habit of forgetting things like telephone numbers and so on, however, this may not be the case for you! It has two wheels and a metal push-pull handle on the side. The price is £109.50 which may seem high, but you are paying for the added security of that combination lock. Our testers thought it was strong but rather heavy, compared to the first two cases.

The last case we tested is definitely in the luxury price range at £199. It's the Mayfair and is sold only by a few specialist stores, mostly in London. It measures 80cm and is made of silver-grey aluminium and if you want a case that really stands out from the rest, this is certainly it! It has two locks, though no combination, two wheels and a push-pull handle on the side. We found that it moved very smoothly and easily in our tests and our verdict is that it's both smart and practical but a bit overpriced.

UNIT 2A

▶ Focus on listening 1 (p. 21)

Now a look at other courses and career opportunities around this week.

For any unemployed people in the Redfield area, why not try a 'Start' course? They'll be running next week, from the 7th to the 11th of May and are free. The organisers can help out-of-work people get going again by giving advice on retraining, voluntary work and possible jobs.

Hurry, hurry if you want to become Young Engineer of the Year. The closing date for this national competition is the end of May and there's a prize of £1,000 for your school or group if your invention is voted the best in the country.

Well, now to the jobs around this week ... And in Taunton there's a job for a trainee sales person aged between 16 and 18 on business machines. You need a driving licence, either provisional or full – it doesn't matter which – and the pay's £3,000 a year.

In Wells there's a job for two experienced grooms. You'll have to work with four horses in a small showjumping yard. The pay is £40 for a six-day week plus expenses.

At Warmley, there are jobs for twenty shop assistants for a new fruit and vegetable store opening in June. There are five full-time and fifteen part-time vacancies. You've got to be over sixteen and the pay's just over £2 an hour.

And you've got to be an early riser for this next one! It's a trainee baker at Easton. You'll start at six in the morning and they'll pay between £55 and £65 a week.

That's all for this week. The number to ring for any further information is 693217. And happy job hunting!

▶ Focus on listening 2 (p. 27)

A = Interviewer   B = John

A   Now, when did you join the Merchant Navy?
B   I joined in 1956.
A   How old were you then?
B   Sixteen.
A   Why did you do it?
B   I joined because all my family were in the Merchant Navy. My father and all my uncles were merchant seamen, and my brother joined when he was 16, so it was a sort of assumption that I would join the Merchant Navy as well, and it was an idea that I went along with. I never thought of anything else.
A   How did it actually start? I mean, where did you ... first join a ship?
B   I joined a ship first of all in Tilbury, which is in Essex, after doing six months' training in a ... a training school. And the first ship I joined – in fact, at the last minute they didn't need me. They had enough crew members. And I actually left the ship just before it sailed. Then I was appointed to another ship and ... that time I actually sailed with it.
A   And you did a six-month course.
B   A six-month course. Yes.
A   What sort of things did that cover?
B   Very basic things like how to lay a table in a first-class dining room, how to carry cups and saucers and plates when the ship was moving around. But really probably the most important thing and probably one of the reasons they did it was to see whether you were up to being away from home in rather difficult conditions. Because it was a former women's prison that the school was situated in. So it was very spartan with rather ... er ... strict discipline, that sort of thing.
A   So what was your title when you first went to sea?
B   When I first went to sea, I was a bellboy.

A Would that involve serving as well?

B Well, mainly bellboys used to stand by the bellboard, and then, when one of the bells rang, they went with a silver tray to find out what people wanted.

A How long did you do that for?

B You go up in a series of ranks and the bellboy rating lasts for two years, from the age of 16 to 18.

A And in that first two years did you ever question what you were doing?

B No, never. It never occurred to me. I was too busy enjoying myself, I think.

A Did you ever question your life?

B I only questioned what I was doing when other people questioned me. If somebody said 'You're wasting your time. You could be leading a normal life instead of this sort of gipsy existence of going from place to place all the time.' But it was only for a second because I was earning quite a lot of money and seeing an awful lot of the world.

A How long were you at sea in all?

B I was there till 1962.

A Six years.

B And then I went back to the Merchant Navy for another four years later on.

A Was there ever anything you found really hard to put up with?

B One of the most difficult things was the fact that the living quarters were very poor. And ... em ... the first ship I was on, there were fourteen boys in a cabin, and ... em ... that meant you only had iron bunks and tin drawers that were put underneath the bunks. That was the only furniture in the place, no carpets on the floors, just bare floors. And ... that was a bit grim because, although I must say most of my shipmates were very nice and very good to get on with – if you found somebody that you didn't get on with, it was very difficult because you couldn't get away from them.

A Were you ever in danger – in a dangerous situation?

B Well, it was rather rough on some of those ships. I mean inside the ship if not on the sea! Storms, yes. There was one particular time when the ship ran into a typhoon as we were going into Hong Kong. We weren't allowed into the harbour because it ... em ... the weather was so bad that the ship would've been smashed up against the quay. And I do remember seeing all the heavy anchor chain and such like swept off the front of the ship by a wave, and thinking – well, if you went into the sea in this weather, nothing could save you. We did in fact go in about a day later, into Hong Kong, through into the harbour, and ... em ... I remember there was a ship that had actually been washed up on to the quay. You could actually walk under the bows of the ship!

A Gosh, that must've been quite a storm! What made you decide to leave in the end?

B I left in the end because I'd finally been convinced by people that it was time I did something else. That was really what happened. I mean I would probably have gone on otherwise.

A And did you find another job straight away?

B Well, I went to Australia for six years, I lived there, and then eventually I came back to England and started a completely new career, as you know. But that's another story!

UNIT 3A

▶Focus on listening 1 (p. 35)

A = Presenter   B = Liz Jones
C = Bruce McCarthy   D = Barbara Bowen

A Good afternoon. In our programme today, we're going to look at two sports – one well-established, one relatively new. We're also going to hear about those little green birds which most of us have kept as pets at one time or another, but which are a very serious hobby to some people.

Our first report comes from Liz Jones and she's been finding out about the sport of judo.

B Hello. Yes well, I've been visiting a local judo club and I've discovered that judo takes its name from the Chinese term for 'gentle way' though you might not think so when you see the way the club members throw each other about!

Apparently, a Dr Jigoro Kano collected knowledge from the old Japanese samurai jujitso schools and then founded the first judo school in 1882. The sport has become popular throughout the world in the last 20 years and there is now an International Judo Federation with its headquarters in Pa ●. In 1964, judo was first included as an event in the Olympic games.

The best advice for anyone wanting to take up judo is to contact their nearest large club for information about courses. Membership fees are usually between £16 and £18. You'll need a judo suit and these cost about £15 to buy. You can also hire one from a club for about £5 a month.

A Thank you Liz. And from a sport with an ancient history to one of the world's newest sports – windsurfing. Our reporter is Bruce McCarthy.

C Windsurfing is very simple to describe, but, as I've been discovering, not so easy to do! You first need to learn to balance on a very slim board. Once you've got the hang of that, you have to struggle with a sail that seems to have a mind of its own! Naturally, while you're learning, you fall into the water over and over and over again. And I've got very wet hair to prove it! It's a sport that was invented in 1969 in California (where falling in is a lot more fun, I should think). In 1984 it became an Olympic event and nowadays there are growing numbers of enthusiasts – an estimated 100,000 in Britain, in fact.

If you feel like joining them, you can take a course at a school for between £30 and £40. A beginner's board will cost you around £300 if you decide to buy your own. And, if you really get hooked, a smart racing board will cost at least £1,000.

In Britain the season for windsurfing is from March to September. If you are determined to keep it up during the winter, you'll need a dry suit which you can wear over your ordinary clothes.

A Thanks, Bruce. Now, finally on to that item on a very familiar pet – the budgerigar. Barbara Bowen has been talking to people who keep not one or two but dozens!

D Yes, budgies have come a long way since they were first introduced into this country from Australia around 1840. Nowadays, it's estimated that 1 in 20 households in the UK owns a pet budgerigar, mostly bought from the local pet shop for around £7. Serious budgerigar breeders, on the other hand, will pay £500 for a really successful show bird.

If you're tempted to become a budgerigar breeder, do be warned that although budgies make good tame pets when they're kept singly, they can be quite aggressive when they are mixed together in a group. Most breeders belong to a local society and there's also the Budgerigar Information Bureau which can offer advice on pets and how to breed them. Their telephone number is 01 (if you're outside London) 127 3444. Breeders aim to produce birds of outstanding shape and colour so as to catch the judge's eye at a show. The one bird every breeder would like to be able to produce is a true pink budgerigar but, so far, no one has succeeded!

A Well that's all for today. Hope you can join us next week.

▶ Focus on listening 2 (p. 42)

A = Presenter   B = Ned Saunders

A Like a lot of businessmen, Ned Saunders has recently become a lot more concerned about fitness. He started running regularly about two years ago and his current ambition is to run in the next London Marathon.

Ned travels a lot in his work as a Sales Manager and when he attends meetings away from home, he likes to keep up his running while exploring new places at the same time. Last month he was in the city of Bristol for a conference and here he is, describing the route he took on an early morning run.

B I set out to run about five miles on that occasion. It was a typical British summer day – wet and windy! I started from my hotel which was next to the floating harbour and ran up to the statue of Neptune in the City Centre. There I turned sharp left, and keeping the floating harbour on my left, ran past the shops and a boat called the Lochiel which is now a floating restaurant. I then carried on along the north side of the harbour until I was almost opposite the Great Britain, you know – the famous iron ship designed by the engineer Brunel. It's been almost completely restored now and looks magnificent.

At that point, I was forced to turn inland by the road layout. I decided I'd had almost enough of the waterfront anyway, so I headed up Jacob's Wells Road – a gentle climb which forced me to slow down to a jog. The map suggested I needed to go further west so, half way up, I took the first turning on the left – a steep hill as it turned out. Perhaps if I'd realised how steep it was, I'd have found an alternative route! Anyway, by the time I'd struggled to the top I almost stopped off at the nearby Chesterfield Hospital to recover my strength!

The going got easier after that. I carried on past the hospital and took the second turning on the left which led into the heart of pretty Clifton village. From the end of the street, I had a marvellous view of another of Brunel's achievements, the Clifton Suspension Bridge. I fancied going over it and coming back but, as I don't normally carry any money with me when I'm out running, the 2p fee kept me from doing so. Anyway, after I'd stood at the entrance and looked across, I turned round and headed back to town. All downhill and easy going now, I thought.

I passed Clifton Down and ran into Clifton Park. From there I turned right and crossed a busy junction to Richmond Hill. That took me into Queen's Road with all its shops and past the City Museum and Art Gallery. When I reached the University tower, I branched right down Park Street to the City Centre once more.

At the bottom of the hill, it was left past the Hippodrome which had a production of The Sound of Music. Then, turning left off the centre, up Colston Street, takes you past the Colston Hall. As Colston Street was taking me uphill again, it seemed as good a time as any to think about turning back. So, it was down Christmas Steps with its little medieval shops and then a dash across the dual carriageway and back via St Stephen's Street to the hotel and a hot bath.

I had been out precisely 43 minutes, including a couple of map reading stops. At a fairly leisurely pace and with a couple of steep hills, about five miles, as I had intended. One of the nicer city runs I've done because there is so much of interest to see in Bristol, even if it is hilly!

UNIT 4A

▶ Focus on listening 1 (p. 50)

A = Presenter   B = Detective

A And now we come to the part of our programme where we ask you, the viewer, to help in the fight against crime. Here, to bring us up to date on crime in our area, as usual, is John Haddrell of Wessex CID. Hello John.

B Hello again. Well, first let me thank the viewers for their first class response to our appeal for information last week. You may remember that we told you how thieves had stolen musical instruments belonging to the Barrington Youth Orchestra. Well, I'm glad to say that, thanks to you, those young musicians have got most of their instruments back now.

A Yes, l know you can't tell us too much at the moment, John, but what are the details you can give?

B Well, we managed to locate two flutes, two recorders and a trumpet, following a telephone call from a viewer. Then, a few days later, some more information helped us to trace the rest of the items, with the exception of the drum, which is still missing. Anyway, we're questioning several people at present and we're hopeful of bringing charges quite soon.

A So, on to this week's cases. In the early hours of Monday morning, thieves broke into Bell's toyshop in Regents Road. They took a number of items including a child's bicycle and this doll you can see on your screens now. Is there anything special about it, John?

B Yes, it may look like an ordinary doll but it's actually quite valuable because it's computer-controlled and it's one of only a handful in the country. It's made by an American company and it's got the maker's name 'Computatrix' printed on its back.

A So, if anyone offers you a doll like this at a bargain price, have a look at the back, and if you see that name, get in touch with your local police station. We know the thieves got away in a stolen green van, don't we John? Can you tell us anything about that?

B Well, we still haven't found the green van but we know it was like the one you can see in this picture and the registration was MUG 335J. One other thing, one of the thieves dropped his chequebook and we're hoping that will help us to trace him quite quickly.

A Still on the subject of people who are careless, £5,000 worth of photographic equipment was stolen from Zoom's in the High Street, but look what they left behind!

B Yes, they left the tools they used behind them. You can see some of the items on your screens now. There's a file, a spanner and a rather unusual hammer. Perhaps that'll help to jog someone's memory.

A You're pretty certain that there were three young men involved, aren't you?

B Yes, we've got a pretty good idea that there were three of them, all in their twenties, and we think they were driving a white saloon car of some type but we haven't got any more information on that, I'm afraid.

A Now what about the things they stole?

B Yes, well, they took several cameras, one of which was worth over £1,000. You can see a similar model on your screens now and we're obviously particularly keen to find that. They also got away with quite a lot of professional equipment including tripods, flashguns and telephoto lenses. But the shop also stocks a range of binoculars and telescopes, and the thieves picked one very powerful telescope to add to their haul.

A Well, that's it for this week. If you think you have any information which might help the police to clear up either of the crimes we've told you about, please get in touch with your local police station. Thanks John. See you next week.

▶ Focus on listening 2 (p. 53)

A = Reporter   B = Alan Higgins

A Imagine that you had just got married and then, even before the honeymoon had started, you had your passport, chequebook and all your luggage stolen! What a disaster, you might say. Well, that's exactly what happened to poor Alan and Cheryl Higgins from Southampton. And now they've had to abandon their honeymoon and stay at home in order to sort out all that problems. Earlier today I talked to Alan on the phone and asked him to tell me what happened.

B Well, we were on our way up to the airport to catch a flight to the Canary Islands, where we were going for our honeymoon. And as we had a bit of time in hand, we decided to stop off at Stratford-on-Avon to have a look around. So we parked the car and went for a walk along the river. We can't have been gone for more than 20 minutes, I should say. And when we got back to the car, it had all gone – our two suitcases, and the flight bag which had our airline tickets and passports in it – everything! Oh, and just to make matters worse, the flight bag also had my credit card and our new chequebook in it.

A How did you feel when you saw what had happened?

B I just couldn't believe it. To be honest, I thought it was a joke at first. I thought some of my friends must have followed us up to Stratford and taken the stuff out of the car as a joke. I was expecting someone to jump out from behind a tree, laughing their heads off.

A Where had you left your bags?

B They were all under a blanket. I'd put that over them to hide them. Maybe it just drew the thief's attention to them. But I can't really understand how anybody could do it. I mean, it was obvious that we had just come from a wedding because the car was covered with coloured streamers and someone had written 'Just married' on the back window.

A And when you realised it wasn't a joke, what did you do then? Well, actually, your father's a senior policeman, isn't he, so I suppose you would have known exactly what to do!

B Yes, well we went to the police in Stratford and they were very sympathetic. We gave them all the details but there wasn't much they could do, of course.

A I can see why someone would steal a chequebook but what would they do with your clothes?

B The police said that he'd probably try to sell some of them and then just throw away what he couldn't get any money for.

A Did you have a lot of clothes stolen?

B Yes. All my clothes went. I haven't got anything to wear now except a winter coat. Not much use on a June honeymoon in the Canary Islands!

A What happened then?

B Well, we had to drive back home so as to deal with the insurance and things.

A It can't have been much fun, when you should have been on your honeymoon!

B No, and the trouble is that when something like that happens, you begin to feel afraid even in your own home. But anyway, as Cheryl – my wife – works in a bank, she was able to sort out the problems about the stolen chequebook and the credit cards quite easily. And then we went to the travel agent's, and I must say they were really marvellous. They managed to fix us up with another holiday in Rhodes in about two weeks' time.

A Oh, so you will be having a honeymoon after all, even if it isn't in the Canary Islands.

B Yes, thanks to them.

A Even so, it must have been an awful experience. How does Cheryl feel about it now?

B Well, she was pretty upset to begin with but now, especially now that the stolen chequebook and credit card have been dealt with, she's a lot happier.

A What a way to start a marriage! After this, are you afraid you're in for a difficult time as a married man?

B Oh no. After all, things can only get better after this! No, it's marvellous to be married.

UNIT 5A

▶Focus on listening 1 (p. 62)

Today we continue our short series about the consumer society with a look at the life-spans of modern products.

Even the best of products wear out in time, of course, but there is a great temptation for manufacturers to design a product so that it wears out quickly even though it could last for years. When our electric light bulb comes to the end of its life after, say, 200 hours, we buy another and the company makes a profit. Bulbs used in factories and industry, however, last much longer and there's no reason why a household bulb shouldn't too.

When things don't wear out fast enough, manufacturers try to persuade customers to buy the latest model by advertising a new style, colour or extra improvements. Of course, real improvements in the design and working of a product are to be welcomed. Very often, however, so called improvements are only minor adjustments or just gimmicks to make you feel that your car or washing machine is out of date. The fashion and car industries have been most successful at this game of introducing new models on a regular basis. But manufacturers of household goods and furniture have been trying to cash in too. If manufacturers have their way the kitchen of tomorrow will be bought as a single unit. There will be yearly model changes and a range of colour schemes so that your kitchen matches the disposable chairs, plates and cutlery you'll be using in it!

In the developing world, the story is rather different. Products which we take for granted are scarce and they have to last much longer. If they break or break down, they are patched or repaired to keep them going for as long as possible.

Washing machines and irons, for example, are designed by their makers to have a useful life of 5 years and that is the length of time that they are normally used for in the USA. In underdeveloped countries, however, they go on being used for 5 times as long – for 25 years, in fact.

Another example is that of cars. They are designed to last 11 years but in America they are replaced with a newer model after an average of only 2.2 years. In the third world they are often kept going for 40 years or more.

The figures for bicycles are even more astonishing. Bicycles, like cars, are only used for about 2 years even though they are designed by their makers to have a useful life of 25 years. In developing countries bicycles are so valuable that they go on being used for up to 75 years!

In the case of another vital product, construction equipment, the makers estimate that this will have an average useful life of 14 years. In the USA it is usually replaced after only 8 years but in the third world, construction equipment is still in use in many places after 100 years or more.

Ships are kept in use for almost as long – 80 years in fact, in the third world, compared with America where they have a working life of only 15 years – just half the time they are designed to last by their manufacturers.

A final example is that of photographic equipment which is designed to last for 35 years and continues to be used for 50 in underdeveloped countries. The shocking fact is that Americans replace their cameras and other equipment after an average of just over one year, or 1.1 years, to be exact!

I think these figures speak for themselves. The fact is that a small proportion of the total population is using too many of the world's resources and using them terribly wastefully. The situation can't continue for ever because the world's resources are shrinking fast.

▶ **Focus on listening 2** (p. 69)

A = American tourist   B = Tourist information officer

Part one

A I'm a visitor to Britain and I'm very interested in your national parks. I'd like to ask you a few questions about them if I may.

B Well, I'll do my best to answer them.

A How many are there altogether?

B Ten.

A And how were they originally set up?

B Well, during the Second World War people were getting more and more interested in the idea of national parks. The first national parks had been created in the United States back in the 19th century, as you probably know ...

A Yeah, I'm from California myself.

B And that had created worldwide interest. So after the war the government finally acted and a law was passed in 1949 to create a new body called the National Parks Commission.

A And were all the ten parks created at that time too?

B No. The first four were set up two years later in 1951. Then more were added up until 1957, when the last national park was created.

A And what kind of places are they, these national parks? I mean, in the States they're pretty wild, but I guess you don't have any real wildernesses in Britain.

B No, very few. But they are all very different. To give you some idea, perhaps I'd better describe one or two.

A I'd appreciate that. I'm hoping to get to see some during my visit.

B Well, let's take the Lake District which is the best known ...

A Sure, I've heard of that.

B It's the largest of the national parks and it's got some marvellous lake and mountain scenery – including Scafell Pike which is the highest mountain in England. It's very popular with visitors especially as some of the lakes can be used for sailing, canoeing and swimming, and the mountains are ideal for rock climbing.

A What about the Peak District? It's shown right in the middle of the map I have here. It sounds like there are mountains there too.

B Well, no – despite the name, there aren't many peaks there in fact. There are really two Peak Districts – the White Peak and the ...

A Why's it called that?

B Oh, it's called the White Peak because of the white-coloured limestone. And then there's also the Dark Peak which is more dramatic but still beautiful. The Peak District gets about 2 million visitors a year, you know, which makes it the most heavily-used of all the national parks.

A Is there a special reason for its being so popular?

B Well, as I said, it is very beautiful, but I think it's also because just about half the population of England lives within a day trip of the Peak District, so it's quite easy to get to.

A I see. Which is the smallest of the parks?

B The Pembrokeshire Coast is. It's in the south-west of Wales – can you see it on the map? It's also the most densely populated of the parks. It's a really beautiful coast – I'd recommend you to go there. It's got a mild climate and there are lovely walks along the cliff tops.

A OK – you've persuaded me! And if I decide to head for Wales, I guess I could also go to the Snowdonia National Park. What is there to see there?

B Well, Snowdon of course! That's the highest mountain in England and Wales, and well worth a visit. But there's lots more. It's got beaches, too, as you can see from the map, and forests, lakes and waterfalls. There are quite a number of historic houses and castles ...

A Castles?!

B Oh yes, and old mines too if you're interested in industrial archaeology.

A Great! I have to go there. Now tell me about Northumberland. That's on the border with Scotland, isn't it?

B Yes, and it's in one of the most remote areas of the country. You can wander for miles and hardly ever see another person.

A But isn't Hadrian's Wall in Northumberland? I've heard that's quite something.

B Yes, that's in the south of the park and that's where most of the visitors go. It was a wall built by the Romans to keep the Scots out and it's a very important and impressive site.

Part two

A Well, thank you for all that information. One last question: can you explain those signs on the wall to me? There are ten of them so I guess they must represent the ten national parks.

B That's right. Most of them are designed to show some special feature of the park. For example, the one with the pony on it ...

A Pony? Which is that? My eyes aren't too good.

B Can you see? – the one shaped like a diamond – with a black pony, a small horse, on it.

A Oh yes – now which park is that for?

B That's the sign for Dartmoor because of the famous Dartmoor ponies which wander over Dartmoor. Exmoor, on the other hand, has a lot of wild deer and the sign for Exmoor shows a stag's head. It's that triangular one over there. Can you see it?

A The triangular one, you say? Right! I've got it.

B Yes, and you can see the stag's head with its wide antlers branching out on top. Now can you see the white bird on a black background?

A Yeah, I can see a bird – with long wings – flying. What is it? An eagle?

B I'm not sure, to tell you the truth. Anyway it's the sign for the Northumberland National Park.

A Northumberland? That's one I'm planning to go to. Tell me, is that some kind of sheep – there in that square sign?

B Yes it is. Well, it's meant to be a ram's head actually! It's the sign for the Yorkshire Dales, because Yorkshire is great sheep-rearing country. Can you see the ram's fine curling horns?

A Sure. Now, that one with a mountain – is that the sign for the, er, Lake District?

B Which one with a mountain? There are two ...

A The circular one – there's a mountain in the distance and, I guess it's a lake, in front.

B Correct! It's the Lake District. But can you guess what the one with the fire is?

A Let me see ... fire ... no, wait a minute. It's not the Brecon Beacons, is it?

B You're absolutely right! Well done! As you know, beacons were fires lit at the top of hills as a kind of signal, and hills where that happened are sometimes called 'beacons' too.

A OK. That makes sense. But the one that really foxes me is that thing like modern art. The one with the circle on the rectangle. What on earth is that supposed to represent?

B I'm afraid I'm as baffled as you are. I can tell you it's the sign for the Peak District.

A Well, thanks again. I won't take any more of your time but I've learned a lot today, and I'm looking forward to seeing a couple of national parks for myself! By the way, if you're ever in California, I can recommend the Yosemite National Park!

UNIT 6A

▶ Focus on listening 1 (p. 77)

C = Reporter A = Anne Evans
B = Nigel Floyd D = Jack Daniels E = Mary Silver

A As far as I'm concerned, it's about the third worst thing that's happened in my life. I can't – I honestly can't imagine anything worse, except illness or death!

B I've never lived through a more terrible moment in my life. It was then about midnight and I was alone in the house. I simply sat in the chair and covered my head with a cushion and wished I were a long way away where no one could find me.

C What on earth was the tragic disaster in these people's lives? The end of their marriage? The loss of their job? Had the dog run away? Actually, they're all writers and they'd lost extremely important work in their word processors. And, as Nigel Floyd, the cookery writer explains, when your computer lets you down, it can be just as bad as a broken love affair!

B I'd finally got round to investing in a word processor and it had taken me quite a bit of time to get used to it. But it was proving really useful and I began to think of it as an old friend! I was about half way through the book when I decided to change one of the recipes. So I put in the disk and found the place. Then, without thinking, I pressed the key but it must have been the wrong one because, instead of just deleting part of the recipe, the whole disk was wiped clean and I had lost 50 recipes, about five day's work. I couldn't believe it. And after that, I'm afraid I went back to my old typewriter – much more reliable!

C And as journalist Anne Evans explains, pressing the wrong key is not the only thing that can destroy your work ...

A I'd just got back from New York and I was writing an article which was going to be a main feature in the newspaper I work for, a world exclusive in fact. I only had the night to write it – the deadline was in the morning. I worked all night in my office on an Astra computer. And I got the article finished! Then, at 7 o'clock in the morning, in comes the cleaning lady, takes out the plug and puts in her vacuum cleaner! This cut of all the electricity and all my work had gone! The whole article! I had two hours before the deadline ...

C Just switch off the electricity or press the wrong button and your trusted work mate can change into a technological monster! Here, with another horror story, is novelist, Jack Daniels.

D I was working on a novel which was giving me quite a lot of trouble. I'd been correcting and rewriting the first two chapters for nearly a month, using my old Rocket 22. Anyway, finally I finished the first two chapters – very late. Then I decided to copy what I'd written on one disk on to another, for safe keeping. I pressed the right key – no question about that – and then I thought I'd just check to make sure the machine had copied what I wanted it to copy. And, to my horror, I found that it had stored only some of my very early notes, and the rest of my work – two whole chapters – had been completely lost. It was the absolute end!

C But even without errors and malfunctions, your life's work is still not entirely safe stored in a computer. As Mary Silver, the television reporter, tells us.

E I'd been doing research for a very long and very important television documentary on the American elections. I'd spent several weeks travelling in the States, interviewing people, and I had an enormous amount of material. I'd completed three days' very intensive work of putting together historical details and facts and statistics, and it was nearly finished. Anyway, I was working late one night and I felt I just couldn't do any more, so I decided to give myself four hours' sleep, so I went to bed. Everybody was in – my husband, the three children. And, er, I came down at about seven in the morning to find broken glass everywhere. It was obvious what had happened. And my word processor had disappeared. And with it had disappeared my entire script for the documentary.

C And what was your reaction?

E Well, absolute horror! I couldn't understand why they'd stolen the word processor because the only other thing they'd taken was a frozen chicken from the freezer, and I couldn't see the connection between the frozen chicken and the American elections!

▶ Focus on listening 2 (p. 81)

A = Presenter B = Child 1 C = Child 2
D = Child 3 E = Child 4 F = Child 5 G = Child 6

A Twenty years ago we asked a group of thirteen-year-olds what they thought life would be like in the year 2000. And this is what they said ...

B In the year 2000, I think I'll probably be in a spaceship on my way to the planet Mars. Or else I may be in charge of a robot court, judging some robots. Or I may be at the funeral of a computer. Or, if something's gone wrong with someone's nuclear bombs, I may be coming back to my cave from a hunting trip!

C I think the population will have gone up so much that either everyone will be living in big plastic domes in the Sahara desert or else they'll be living under the sea.

D Computers are taking over now. Computers and automation. And in the year 2000 there just won't be enough jobs to go around.

A Well that was before the manned moon landing, the micro-processor and test-tube babies. So, have the hopes and fears of today's thirteen-year-olds changed as they look forward to the year 2020? We asked a second group of children and here are some of their answers.

E Obviously nuclear war worries me, but I don't think that'll happen. Unless they've got computers that press the button for them. Because I don't think that any human being can – is capable of actually pressing some button that releases all the nuclear arms. 'Cos it would just mean the destruction of the world.

F Perhaps we'll be able to convert brain waves into radio waves and then change them back to brain waves, so you could actually have a conversation with someone without talking. But you'd have to be able to stop them understanding some of your thoughts I suppose in case they got upset! And there'll be so many people – I think there may – unless they have another planet to go to – there'll be loads and loads of tower blocks for people to live in, or people will be restricted to a certain number of kids.

G It'll probably be computers that are running the country by then. I mean they're beginning to now and that can be a good thing. But when it comes to war and things like that – nuclear bombs, and they're designing gases that can kill people within seconds. I think that aspect of technology should be wiped out completely.

A Amazing, isn't it? Twenty years later and yet the issues remain the same.

UNIT 1B

▶Focus on listening 1 (p. 90)

A = Interviewer   B = Prospective traveller

A Just tell me what happens, then. You set off, on Thursday, in a coach, a car …?

B Well, you go by coach to Dover and then on the other side, they've got a, the company has specially converted double-decker buses.

A Oh really?

B So the bus picks you up, at Calais I think it is, and then you go on the bus all the way to Kathmandu. So it takes about ten weeks.

A And what's the route actually?

B Um – you go down through Europe to … well, you go through Venice and then down through Greece and Turkey, um, and then from Turkey you go down through Syria and Jordan. Then you go back up through Syria and Jordan again and back into Turkey. And from Turkey you go to Iran and then you go across Iran and, um, into Pakistan. And up through northern India and finally into Nepal. You go to Kathmandu and stay there for about a week or ten days.

A U – hum. And did you have to get all the visas for the various places?

B Well, I had to get three. I had to get an Australian visa, an Indian visa and an Iranian visa.

A Do you have to have supplies of money for each place? – I mean local currency?

B Well no. What I've done is just to get a lot of traveller's cheques – plus they advise you to take some dollars in cash because, well, that's acceptable currency in a lot of places. So it's just a case of changing the money as you get into a new country.

A And do you sleep on the bus?

B Yeah. They've converted the top deck so you sleep there. And downstairs there's seating and, um, a sort of kitchen.

A And how rough is it?

B I don't think it's too bad. They've got bunk beds with mattresses and you take a sleeping bag. And I think the hotels they provide are quite adequate. There are quite a few overland companies and with a lot you have to camp every night. Well, I mean camping's fine for a couple of weeks, but four months! And having to travel all day and then stop and pitch tent! At least this way, if you get tired during the day, you can just go upstairs and have a lie down.

A Do you know anyone who's going?

B No.

A Is there an age limit?

B Yes, 35. It's 18 to 35.

A Do you get a lot of information before you go?

B Oh, yes. They send you a list of things you should do, about how to get the visas and about your injections because you have to have lots of vaccinations, and what clothes to wear …

A Well, you can't take much luggage, can you?

B No, well I've just got a fairly small travel bag and I'll take a rucksack as well, so that, um, I can pack everything in and I've also got some space for souvenirs and things.

A So you sleep on the bus all the way to Kathmandu, and then you stay in a …

B Hotel. Yes. After Kathmandu, it's a mixture of buses and planes and trains. It's all local transport and you stay in hotels.

A I see.

B You actually fly from Kathmandu to Burma.

A Well, how much does it all cost?

B Well – the actual trip from London to Australia costs just over £2,000. It seems a lot but it's for four months' travel and that includes your hotel accommodation. Well, all your accommodation. And transport, and food. So really all you've got to take is your spending money.

A What made you want to do it?

B Well, I've always wanted to go round the world and before now I've never really had the money. I've been working for the last few years so I've managed to save up the money and I thought it's a good time to do it. I'm not too young and I'm not too old and …

A How old are you?

B I'm twenty-four. I don't own a house or anything like that, that it might be difficult to leave behind. And I just thought I might as well do it now while I've got the chance.

A It's very brave! And what will you do in Australia?

B I don't know but I've got some friends in Brisbane I'm going to stay with and I've got a work permit for six months so I might be able to pick up some work. Um. So I really just want to have a look around. I'd like to go to New Zealand as well.

A Well it all sounds fantastic! I'm quite envious actually – anyway, best of luck and don't forget to send me a postcard.

B I won't.

▶Focus on listening 2 (p. 97)

A = Interviewer   B = David Hempleman-Adams

A Well, I've been looking forward to meeting you and I'm longing to ask you about your walk to the North Pole. It was, well tell me, was it three years ago that you went?

B The first expedition was to the geographical North Pole and that was 1982 and that was a couple of years' planning, so the initiation of that first expedition was probably 1980 and then it took a long time to plan it, and then we finally left England in 1982 and got up into the north of Canada in February.

A Sorry, was that the first trip or the second?

B The first trip.

A The first trip, yes. Did that … was that successful?

B No. We … at the time, I got to 87°11′ and I cracked three ribs and I gave up after … um … a bit of soul searching. And it was a bit disappointing in some respects because there'd been a lot of planning and although we failed … it was good in the sense that we did so well because everyone said we'd be … or I would be dead in six days because of the cold, and so it was interesting that I actually succeeded in living in those conditions for 42 days and actually achieved about three quarters of the distance. And at that time it was the furthest anyone had attained, getting to the North Pole without dogs or snowmobiles.

A Yes. After that first one, didn't it put you off starting again to do a second visit?

B Yes, um … At the time … it's like anything that … which, when you're in conditions where you're extremely frightened and it's dangerous, you feel what on earth are you doing here, I mean, it's crazy and every minute I hated it but when I was home, I missed it completely – so it was something that I had to get back to, and as the months passed, I – I wanted to get back, … and try it again. At that stage I was trying to emulate what had happened in the Himalayas, and that was small alpine expeditions, they're becoming smaller and smaller on big mountains. And that culminated in Ronald Messner climbing Everest solo without oxygen and that to me was the purest form of …

A So that's what attracts you really, is the refining it to its simplest form?

B Yes, well, in this day and age, I mean, I've been born in the twentieth century and unfortunately everything's been explored … um … so really the only thing that's left to myself and other explorers … is to try and do it better or faster or on less money, or more refined, as you say. There'd always been these massive dog teams – twenty or thirty dog teams … and airplane support which used to cost millions of pounds, in fact, and to me there was no correlation between the amount of money that you paid into an expedition and the success of it. So

I thought, well, what's the point of spending millions and not succeeding, if you could do it in a lightweight fashion – just go with a sledge, without dogs or air support – it would be cheaper and if you failed then you could have another go.

A Yes.

B So I failed the first time and that was with air support . . . I was having a drop every twelve or sixteen days. The second expedition, I wanted to go back and try and push it a stage further and try and be the first person to reach the North Magnetic Pole but that would be in, again, the purest form of travel, without the use of dogs or snowmobiles, but in addition without any air support whatsoever. So everything that I took . . . that was, um, completely a survival kit for myself. And the second expedition, I was very fortunate, um . . . and I . . . with the experience of the first expedition, I achieved that trip.

A And . . . did you have any really frightening moments during this trip?

B I think every day was frightening because at the end of the day, you didn't know if you were ever going to get home . . .

A Um . . . no, what about polar bears?

B Well, . . . the first trip I saw one but I didn't actually have any problems. But I had this theory that on my second trip, because I was coming down – it was a bit further south – and I was going through migration routes for polar bears . . . and we knew polar bears liked Mars bars, so what I did, I used to put a sledge about 20 feet away from the tent in line with the tent flap, and put Mars bars on top of the sledge. And one night, I was asleep and I heard this rustling and this polar bear was after the Mars bars and . . . the next thing I know, it was rolling me out of the tent, and . . .

A Sorry, why did you put the Mars bars out?

B Well, I knew that if it went for the Mars bars first that would give you a couple of seconds to wake up and try to get your gun because, I mean, two or three seconds was crucial. And so this thing came straight for the tent while I was trying to get out of it, and . . . I shot a . . . there's a theory that polar bears are more scared of noise rather than shooting . . . so I shot a round through the floor just to scare it, and it did scare it about twenty feet, and then I gave it another two warning shots, and then it just started to charge, and so I had to try and stop it.

A Really?

B I was really upset by it all, and . . . um . . . seeing this thing coming towards me really unnerved me. And so I got, we got the plane in and sent it back to Resolute and we gave it to the community. They're not endangered at all and they're not protected at all up there. Resolute has a quota of polar bears year they can kill and so it just came off that quota.

A Which upset you? Was it, um, the narrow escape from death or was it shooting the animal?

B Shooting the animal.

A Was it?

B Because I felt it was fair game that he could come after me because I was in his environment and I felt that I was going home after the expedition. But that was his environment and I felt that it was unfair for me to . . . although it's the survival of the fittest, I thought it was a shame because they're beautiful animals and I think that if anyone should appreciate that environment, it's probably polar bears more than, more than me.

UNIT 2B

▶ **Focus on listening 1** (p. 109)

A = Adult   B = Child 1   C = Child 2   D = Child 3

A Right, we'll start with you then. Can you tell . . . can you tell us how old you are?

B Nine.

A Nine. And have you got brothers and sisters?

B Yeh.

A How many?

B Two brothers.

A Two brothers. Are they older than you?

B No, younger.

A What about pocket money? Do you get some pocket money?

B Um, sometimes. We get about . . . off my nan I get about . . . five pounds thirty.

A Five pounds thirty! What, every week?

B No. Three pounds fifty, I mean.

A What, every week?

B Well, most of the time. I don't get it very often, though.

A Um. What do you do with it when you do get it? What do you spend it on?

B I spend it on things like . . . well, sweets and that.

A Is that why one of your teeth has gone, there? Is it?

B Yeh, it's come out.

A And you don't get pocket money from your mummy for helping in the house?

B No, usually my mum gives me about 5p for doing the washing up and laying the table and that.

A And how often do you do that?

B Nearly every day.

A Nearly every day. Who does it when you don't do it, then?

B My ma has to do it, because I'm at school most of the time.

A Ah, do you have to give her 5p then, when she does it?

B No.

A No! Oh. How much pocket money do you think you'd like to have?

B About . . . ten pounds.

A Right. Now, you've got ten pounds a week. What would you spend it on?

B Um . . .

A Not more sweets?

B Um . . . toys.

A And what about when you're naughty? What does mummy do when you're naughty?

B Oh . . . ooh . . . she just sends us up to bed, sometimes.

A Sometimes. And what does she do other times?

B She gives us a smack.

A Oh, does it hurt?

B Mmm

A So you're not naughty very much?

B No. Try not to be.

A Um?

B Try not to be.

A Try not to be. No. What time do you go to bed usually?

B About half past nine.

A Every night?

B Well, on a . . . well, on a Friday and Saturday I go to bed at about eleven o'clock, when my ma goes to bed.

A Oh. Do you watch a lot of television

B Um . . . most of the time, yeh.

A Now, how old are you?

C Seven.

A Seven. Have you got brothers and sisters?

C Yes.

A How many?

C Two.

A What, brothers or sisters?

C One girl and one boy.
A And are they smaller or bigger than you?
C Bigger.
A Oh. And what about your pocket money. How much pocket money do you have?
C Fifty pence.
A Fifty pence. And who gives you that?
C My mum.
A And what do you do with it then?
C Put it in my money box, or spend it on something when I, um, want some sweets or something.
A And would you like to have more pocket money?
C Umm. Ten pound.
A You'd like ten pounds. You're going to have to tell me what you'd spend your ten pounds on.
C I'd like to buy loads and loads of soft toys.
A Would you? And put them all in your bedroom?
C Yeh. I love soft toys.
A Fill your bed up so you can't get in any more? Um. Thought so. What time do you go to bed?
C About eight o'clock or nine o'clock.
A Is it later at the weekends?
C Umm. Yes. Ten o'clock at the weekends.
A Ten o'clock at the weekends.
C Umm. Or nine o'clock.
A And what do you do when you stay up so late? Do you watch television?
C Sometimes. Sometimes I'm still out playing.
A And what about when you're naughty? What happens then?
C I get sent up in my bedroom.
A And who does that most? Mummy or daddy?
C Dad.
A Does he? Oh. And do you have to help in the house?
C Umm. A lot.
A What do you have to do?
C Washing up, dusting, wiping up, putting away, um … and loads more things.
A What happens if you drop mummy's best plates?
C I get sent to bed.
A And what about when you grow up and get married? Do you want to have children?
C Yeh.
A How many would you like to have?
C Six.
A Six! Gosh, you'd need a big house. Why six?
C Oh, don't know.
A Have you found a boyfriend who wants six as well?
C No.

A Right. Can we start by asking you how old you are?
D Eight.
A Eight. And do you live at home with mummy and daddy and brothers and sisters?
D Yes.
A How many brothers and sisters?
D Um, I haven't got any brothers and sisters but I live at home.
A Just you on your own with your mum and dad?
D Yeh, but mum's having a baby in two weeks' time.
A Oooh. Are you excited about that?
D Yes.
A And what about pocket money? Do you get pocket money from your parents?
D Yes.
A How much do you get?
D Um, sometimes I get two pounds, but mostly I get one pound, from all the family.
A And what do you do with it? What do you spend it on?
D Um, toys.
A What sort of toys?
D Um, Care Bears.

A Care Bears? And what do you do with all these Care Bears?
D Um, put them in my bedroom, cuddle them at night.
A All night?
D Yes.
A Umm. And do you think you get enough pocket money?
D Yeh, 'cause my mum said if I had too much I wouldn't know what to buy with it and I agree with her.
A Oh. And do you have to help in the house to get your pocket money, or …?
D No.
A But do you help in the house?
D Sometimes.
A What do you do then?
D Um, lay the table, bring the knives and forks, make some drink …
A And what happens when you're naughty?
D Oh, I get smacked.
A By whom?
D My dad, usually.
A Does it hurt?
D No.
A That's a waste of time then.
D When he's really angry he does.
A I see. So you've got to make him really angry. And what about going to bed? What time do you go to bed?
D Um, my latest is eleven o'clock and my earliest is eight o'clock.
A And what do you do until you go to bed?
D Um, watch the telly and read books.
A And what do you do when you stay up till eleven o'clock.
D Um, it's usually to watch films.
A And if it's eight o'clock and there's a nice film on, do you stay up to watch it?
D No, I usually watch Eastenders, when it's on.
A And then go to bed?
D Yes.
A Good. And what about when you grow and up and get married? Do you want to have children?
D Yes.
A How many would you like to have?
D Two.

▶**Focus on listening 2** (p. 113)

H = Helen   G = Gay

H It's Gay, isn't it?
G Yes. Hallo.
H It's Helen. Do you remember me?
G Yes, yes. Haven't seen you for ages.
H God, it must be years! How are you?
G I'm fine. How are you? You look well.
H Well, I've just been on holiday. What are you doing these days?
G Well, I'm doing some part-time teaching.
H And how's Dick?
G Oh, we're not together any more. He left about three years ago, I'm afraid.
H Oh my God, that must be difficult for you.
G Well, it is sometimes – it's not too bad.
H Have you got any children?
G Yes, I've got a daughter, 13. Gosh! I haven't seen you for a long time! – a daughter, Lily, who's 13, and a 5-year-old boy.
H My God! How do you cope? Have you people around who help you?
G Well, I'm very lucky. I've got a very supportive group of women friends and we share the child care. I mean it's difficult sometimes – when you go out, you've got to pay for going out and pay for a baby-sitter, that sort of thing.
H But what about clothes and shoes? That must be terrible.
G Well, my mother-in-law's very good. She buys the children

shoes. And I don't mind wearing jumble sale clothes and cheap clothes.

H I bet she doesn't buy you clothes! Do you find then that you find it difficult to meet people yourself?

G No, I'm very lucky round here. It's very friendly, and just working part-time is very helpful.

H Where do your family live? Do they live here too?

G Well, no. I've got three brothers – they're all in London. And my father who's 82 is down in Hampshire.

H So you've got to look after him as well?

G Well, I've got to go down about every four weekends or so to see if he's OK. But luckily he's in quite good health. Cheerful. And the kids love going down there.

H How on earth do you manage to make ends meet?

G Well, I get some help. I don't think it's enough really. I think, on the whole, fathers get off rather lightly.

H Because he had quite a good job, didn't he?

G Oh yes, he's a dentist. It's difficult really. If I ask him for more money, it makes things difficult, so I prefer, on the whole, to keep a good relationship with him for the children. They go and spend a night with him once a week, but I don't really think that's doing enough. You know, I have to do all the disciplining and going to parents' evenings and ...

H He buys them ice cream.

G That's right. And he buys them nice expensive presents. So, it's a bit uneven I think.

H So – what kind of teaching are you doing?

G Well, I haven't actually been doing any teaching for six months. I've been doing a wonderful course. It's a wood-machining course.

H A what?

G A wood-machining course. It's been really good fun.

H Whatever's that?

G Well, it's partly funded by central European funds. And it's for women only. And it's been six months and I hope I'm going to set up doing jobs as a wood worker. I've already been asked to make a wardrobe and a plate rack and ...

H What a wonderful idea!

G shelves, and I think it'll be much better than teaching. I really enjoy doing it. It's practical. And the course is so good. You get ...

H Did you have to pay for it?

G No, it was free. And what's even better, there's child care provision built into it. So it means that I can actually, it means that Lily can collect Finn after school on the three days that I've been doing it. And there's money to pay her a reasonable allowance.

H So they pay childcare for you to have a baby-sitter or a child-minder, and you gave it to her instead. That's a good way of keeping the money in the family!

G Well, yes – it means she helps and she doesn't resent helping. Yes, it's been very good.

H I suppose she's quite independent.

G She is. I think on the whole both my children are very independent. I think maybe that's one of the positive aspects of single parenting. I notice that they're very outgoing and they're very easy, they make friends very easily with adults and with other children.

H I suppose they're used to having different child-minders and going to nursery school from when they were quite young?

G Yes, they've never been at all clinging. They've been quite happy to go off and go with other people. They're very independent, both of them.

H Well, that's one good thing that's come out of it then.

G Yes it is.

UNIT 3B

▶ Focus on listening 1 (p. 122)

A = Presenter   B = Expert

A We all know the old saying 'An apple a day keeps the doctor away'. I suppose there's absolutely no truth in that?

B Well, actually I wouldn't say there's no truth in it. It's like a lot of so-called old-wives' tales and advice our grandmothers used to give us – we used to laugh but medical discoveries can prove them right after all. Anyway, apples are certainly a good source of fibre, and fibre, as we now know, is an important element in our daily diet. Apart from that, apples contain Vitamin C which helps build up resistance to disease. So there are some good reasons for eating apples regularly, but I wouldn't like to promise that they'll protect you from all ailments so the saying is a bit of an exaggeration. In any case, there's a great deal more Vitamin C in oranges.

A Right, well what about the advice to always sleep with an open window. I had an uncle who believed it firmly and who stuck to the rule right through the depths of winter!

B Well, I'm afraid that is a myth, and a dangerous one at that. Old people are much more likely to catch infections in extreme cold and that's true of babies too. Cold air can irritate a cough and make life much more uncomfortable for people who suffer from bronchitis. Personally, I wouldn't recommend anyone to leave the window open in cold weather – after all, if you're worried about the bedroom getting stuffy, you can always leave the door open to let the air circulate.

A Yes, well that's good advice. Another thing you often hear is that if you get wet through, you're more likely to catch a cold. I must say I've always believed that.

B Yes, a lot of people do, but actually there's no evidence whatsoever to prove it. There have been experiments both in Britain and America and the results were the same in both countries. Volunteers stayed in damp clothes for some time but they developed no more colds afterwards than their fellow volunteers who had stayed dry. There was also the case of a man in Norway who fell into a freezing river during the spring thaw. He'd spent the winter completely alone – he was a trapper I think. Anyway, he didn't catch a cold as a result, even though he'd had to spend hours in his wet clothes. Then, a few weeks later, he was back in contact with other human beings and he quickly caught a streaming cold!

A Well that's quite surprising, I must say. Another myth bites the dust! Now, what about the saying 'Feed a cold and starve a fever'? I've always found that seems to work.

B Of course it does! People often have quite hearty appetites right through a cold, but when you've got a high temperature you don't feel much like eating. So it's obvious really. On the other hand, if you've got a high 'flu temperature, you need to drink plenty of liquid to replace the fluid you lose through sweating.

A And the last piece of old wives' wisdom I wanted to ask you about is that carrots help you to see in the dark. I seem to remember that someone once died from drinking too much carrot juice, didn't they?

B Yes, that's right but it was a man who drank enormous quantities – more than any normal person would dream of consuming. In fact carrots are a very good source of carotene, and that's a substance which is converted in the body to Vitamin A. Vitamin A is vital because it enables the eye to adapt so that you can see in twilight and darkness. Night blindness is a common symptom of Vitamin A deficiency. There are other good sources of Vitamin A apart from carrots, though – green beans for example, milk, butter and also fish oils.

▶Focus on listening 2 (p. 128)

Well, if everyone's here, perhaps I'd better make a start. The course you're taking is … a … a basic first aid course. We meet once a week on a Tuesday afternoon and the whole course is 20 hours. At the end, you'll take an exam and, if you're successful, you'll get an official certificate to prove that you're a qualified first aider.

As you might expect, there will be a fair amount of practical work during the course because first aid is a subject where a little practical experience is worth a lot of theory! Some of you may be a bit worried about whether you'll be able to put bandages on correctly as you've seen in a first aid handbook. Well, let me reassure you. You can be quite a competent first aider even if you're not very good at putting on bandages. On the other hand, you … you can be … er … a better first aider, shall we say, a more effective first aider, if you're prepared to do the necessary overtime. In other words, to do some extra practice at home following the demonstrations you see during the course.

Now, the first thing you have to remember about first aid, above all else, is this: the need for first aid comes when you least expect it! There are times when extremely fast action can save a life. Now, I'll give you one example of that kind of situation.

I was in a restaurant, having a meal. A gentleman was over there, having a meal. We were taking no notice of each other. Quite suddenly, while I was in the middle of my meal, there was a noise from his table. And I looked over – he'd brought his hands down heavily on the table and he was obviously in some kind of difficulty. I watched him for a moment and he was now leaning forward over the table as if he was in pain. So I got up from my seat and walked across – ten metres, five metres, something like that – to him and noticed, as I got to him, that a section of his false teeth, his denture, was lying at the side of the plate, on the table cloth. And I looked at him and he was now purple, purple! He couldn't breathe. There was something in his throat and it was totally blocking his airway.

By this time, a waiter had come in and said 'What's the matter?' and I said, 'I want to get this man lying across his chair so that he's facing the floor.' So, with the waiter's help, I got him lying over the chair. And I shouted to the waiter 'Call an ambulance! Now'. Because sometimes people get terrified in this kind of situation. They've got to be pushed to know what to do. So he followed my command to go and call an ambulance.

Now, with this man, his airway had to be cleared of the obstruction. I had to get that piece of denture out. Otherwise he was going to die. Now I hit him hard on the back. No denture. Second bang with the flat of the hand between his shoulder blades – no denture. And it was on number seven that the denture came flying out of his mouth. And I didn't have to do the kiss of life. He breathed like an angry bull for about two minutes. You would've found it very disturbing to see that man breathe. But just as the ambulance arrived, he was breathing and he was beginning to come round. They took him away anyway because he needed to be medically examined for any serious results of his experience. But I think he was going to be alright.

Now that's a good example of where you as first aider have got the casualty's life literally in your hands. You are the difference between life and death. And that's not dramatic – that's fact.

At other times, you can find yourself in a far less urgent situation. There's time to stop and think. There's time to consider what to do. This is where you've got to be so careful as a first aider. You've got to recognise what sort of situation it is and, if it's an emergency, act very very quickly.

Oh sorry! I do apologise! Don't please let me do all the talking. Please – I should have said this at the very beginning – interrupt me at any point you like. Is that alright? I would like you to do that.

UNIT 4B

▶Focus on listening 1 (p. 139)

A = Presenter   B = Sam Murphy

A And now we come to the second part of our series 'Young Explorers' and here's Sam Murphy to introduce it.

B Hello. Today we're going to talk about how you can survive if you ever get lost or stranded in the wilds. I'm going to tell you how you can make a shelter and how to collect emergency water. But first, I want to talk about survival kits.

A Are those the kits soldiers and explorers carry – with emergency supplies of food?

B Yes. You may not plan to go to the jungle or desert but a survival kit could still be useful when you're climbing or walking in the countryside. And you don't need to buy a special kit. You can make one yourself from a few odds and ends. I'll explain what you need now so have a pencil and paper ready. The complete kit fits into a matchbox so it's very light and takes up very little room.

A Into a matchbox? That sounds unbelievable, Sam!

B Yes. You'd be surprised what you can get in a matchbox. Why don't you try and see?

A Alright. I've got one here. What do I put in first?

B The first thing is a fishing line. You can buy one from an angling shop or use any piece of nylon thread.

A Does it have to be nylon?

B Yes. Cotton is too weak and it breaks if you catch anything.

A O.K. I've put that in. And to go with the line I expect you need a fishing hook.

B Right! Again you could buy a special fishing hook but a bent pin or nail will do just as well. And next, a razor blade. Be careful, it's sharp!

A What's that for?

B It's for gutting the fish you catch. It's best to use a blade with only one cutting edge if you can find one. They're much easier to handle.

A A blade with one cutting edge. Right. What's next?

B Number four is a plastic bag. Make sure there are no holes in it, though! You'll need the bag for carrying water – and that's essential for survival. You could also use it to cover wounds and protect them from infection, or even as a fishing trap.

A So, a very useful item. I've folded it as small as it will go so as to get it in.

B Good. The next item for the survival kit is a piece of candle.

A To give light?

B Yes. A candle burns more slowly than matches. You can also use candle wax to make things waterproof and I'll say a bit more about that in a minute. And next …

A A balloon! What on earth can you use a balloon for?

B Well, you can use it in the same way as the plastic bag.

A Oh, for carrying water?

B Yes, and to cover wounds. It has the advantage that it will stretch too.

A Isn't there a danger of it stretching too much and bursting?

B Yes, so you must take care because if that happened you could lose valuable water. But even a broken balloon can be useful. You can set light to it and it will help to get your fire going.

A Amazing! Right, I've put that in.

B Next, a needle.

A Is that for sewing?

B Yes, or fishing. But you can also use a needle to make a very simple compass. The instructions are on this week's Fact Sheet and we'll be giving the address for that at the end of the programme. And, now a few matches.

A For lighting a fire?

B Yes. These are the most important part of any survival kit because making a fire is essential and it can take a long time. But before you pack them, you must make them waterproof.

You can use the candle for that. Melt a bit of wax and dip the matches in it.

A And that will prevent the matches from getting damp?

B Yes, and you also find that it helps the matches to burn longer. Now, can you fit this piece of chalk in.

A Just. What's it for?

B For writing messages or marking trees so that you can leave a trail.

A Is that everything?

B Nearly. There is one last item but it doesn't need to go into the matchbox. It's a whistle and you can wear it round your neck on a piece of string. It's useful for calling for help because it takes less effort than banging or shouting and it can be heard further away.

▶ Focus on listening 2 (p. 144)

S = Sue   R = Roger

S The other thing I was going to ask you was if you've still got the map of Morocco. From when we went there – it must be eight years ago now ...

R Should have. I never throw anything away.

S Because Trevor and John are going to Morocco at Easter and I wanted to show them the route we took.

R What – along the coast?

S Well, no. I was thinking of that awful road we took across country. Do you remember? We'd arrived from Spain in the afternoon, hadn't we? And we'd decided to – instead of just staying the night at the port and setting off early ...

R To push on.

S Well, not to push on only, but to drive across half the country! Rabat we were going to. Do you remember?

R Yes.

S And to save time, we thought we'd take that minor road, which looked much more direct.

R Saved miles!

S It was marked yellow on the map, wasn't it – which meant it was suitable for cars.

R Only we didn't realise that it had been an unusually wet spring ...

S And that the rivers, which would normally have been dry, would be in full flood?

R The thing I remember is bowling along happily, first day of the holiday, quite unconcerned. So unconcerned that when that – do you remember that man who jumped into the middle of the road and tried to make us stop ...

S But wasn't it – there were groups of shepherds coming home, weren't there? And as they went past, they shook – they seemed to be shaking their fists at us. And we thought 'The natives are unfriendly!' And it was only later that we realised they were trying to warn us about the river ahead.

R Well in my memory there was only one. But when we came over a hill and saw the river actually flowing across the road ahead of us!

S And the point was that we could've gone back then, but it was getting quite late. And the road had been pretty bad, hadn't it? Very muddy. So we decided to give it a try. You drove the car very fast at it, I remember, and we got through safely. And then we thought we'd made the right decision, and done really well.

R And we thought that was it.

S Yes. And then, a few miles on, we met another river, a bit deeper!

R And by the time we'd ...

S By the time we'd gone through the first one, to go back would've meant going through it again, which we didn't want to risk.

R And even that the car got through safely.

S But when we came to the third river – I'll never forget it! It looked much worse than the other two – a real torrent!

R But we had no choice by then. We had to try and cross it. The worst moment, I remember, was when the engine cut out. The water must have reached the exhaust pipe and it cut out. And then there we were stuck in the middle of this raging river, with our hearts sinking fast. We opened the door, didn't we? And the water came flooding in.

S I opened the door.

R You opened the door. And I remember seeing all our shoes and maps and things bobbing around in the water. It was terrible!

S And the place itself was an absolute wilderness, wasn't it? In the middle of nowhere! That was one of the reasons why our spirits were so low. I mean we sat in the car, in the middle of this river, looked around, and there was no sign of a village or habitation of any kind, as far as the horizon. And yet, being Morocco, in a few minutes this group of children turned up. They ranged from about two to fourteen, didn't they?

R Yes – and they were very cautious. We even had to call them to help us at first. And then they began by pushing from all sides – three or four at the front and three or four at the back! But when we encouraged them to all push in one direction, it worked, eventually. And when the boat – the boat! – when the car was on the bank, we went through our pockets and gave them various ...

S No, we looked through our pockets and we hadn't got a single dirham – is it dirham?

R Dirham.

S Dirham. Because it was our first day and we'd arrived in Ceuta, which is still Spanish, and we hadn't changed any money there.

R But we gave them some Spanish and English coins, which they seemed pleased with. Only then they asked for more, so we actually had to shut the doors and drive away, with them running after us – hoping we wouldn't meet another river!

S Which we didn't, luckily! And then, eventually, we came to the main road. It was such a relief to see all the lights!

R Yes and the car was so wet that we stopped at a service station to empty out the car. Do you remember? We emptied everything out, and in the corner of this hot dusty service station we were scooping out river water all over the forecourt!

S Yes, yes! And then later that night ... in fact it must have been something like three in the morning before we finally got to Rabat. It must have taken a long time to get out of that river!

R Wait a moment and I'll just look for the map. Here it is.

S Oh yes. Let's look. Yes, there's Ceuta, in the north, just opposite Gibraltar at the tip of Spain ... and there's Rabat, on the west coast, down on the left there ...

R Yes, I've got it.

S Now we must have come down to Tetouan ...

R We must have gone through Tetouan.

S Yes. And then ...

R We must have taken that little road to the west, cutting the corner and by-passing Chaoen and Ouezzane.

S Yes, that's where it was – and you can even see the three rivers! Then we must have come to the main road there at Ksar el ... Ksar el Kebir.

R Well be sure to tell Trevor and John to check the weather forecast if they're thinking of following our route!

UNIT 5B

▶ Focus on listening 1 (p. 154)

I don't suppose there are many people who actually enjoy shopping. I mean the daily or weekly shopping trip for food and the other boring, necessary things of life, like soap powder and toothpaste. Up to now, we've had to do our shopping by going to the shops. And after we've queued in the village store or supermarket, we've got to carry our purchases home.

Well now the microchip has come to our aid! Computers are being used to develop shopping systems which will allow us to do our shopping from home. In fact we'll be able to gather information about products, compare prices and buy goods without even leaving the house!

A scheme especially for pensioners was introduced by Gateshead Council earlier this year. It's called the 'Over 60's shopping Line' and it allows elderly people to order anything from a bag of chips to chemist's products from their own homes. They use specially adapted televisions, directly linked by telephone to the council's shopping and information service. At the touch of a button, they can order any one of 1,000 items at the town's main supermarket and a range of other items from the local baker and chemist. The goods are delivered to their home within a few hours and this service is completely free.

A similar scheme in Birmingham was started last year through British Telecom, the company which runs the national telephone service. This scheme is called 'Club 403' and it is available to anyone with a telephone who pays extra for British Telecom's special information service. 'Club 403' allows you to use your telephone to contact the local hypermarket's computer. Information is displayed on your television screen and orders can be placed for any of 10,000 goods stored on the computer. The goods are then automatically delivered to your home.

'Club 403' has proved extremely useful to many a busy working person and parent. Members of the club use their telephone and television set to order groceries, frozen food, fresh food and vegetables, bread and meat. They choose what they want, when they want to have it delivered (day or evening) and the delivery service is free. The only cost to a Club member is £6.50 every three months for the special information service.

For people who live in south London, there's a scheme called 'Shopping Link' which promises all the advantages of a supermarket – such as low costs, variety, freshness and quality, together with a delivery service up to ten o'clock at night. You place your order by telephone but you have to give 24 hours' notice. When the order arrives, you pay £1.73 on top of the bill for the service. You also get a computer printout of your order so you can check off what you've bought.

Finally, there's a scheme called 'Comp-u-card' which is based in Windsor. This system stores information about products in its computer and goods are supplied directly to customers from a nationwide network of manufactures and distributors. Because no actual stock is held, costs are greatly reduced and 'Comp-u-card' offers the lowest prices in Britain! If a customer can prove that a product he or she has bought is available from somewhere else for less money, 'Comp-u-card' will refund the difference to the customer.

This service costs £20 to join and purchases can be made by cheque or credit card.

▶ Focus on listening 2 (p. 158)

I = Interviewer   A = Auctioneer

I   Well, it's ... it's very interesting to meet you, Mr Ewing. I've often wanted to talk to an auctioneer and I wonder, can you tell me how you actually became an auctioneer?

A   Purely by accident, like most things in life ... um ... I joined a firm of chartered surveyors when I came out of Polytechnic, having qualified in fact as a property surveyor, and they happened to have an auction room as part of their business. And I became very interested in that which really revived an interest that I'd had with my family when I was younger, and an opportunity came up to move into the auction side of the business which I took very gratefully, and haven't looked back since.

I   Can I ask you about what people do when they want to make a bid, when they want to offer some money? What's the most usual thing that they do to show you that?

A   Well, the auction obviously is described in a catalogue which is normally just a very rough-printed paper, um, description, and that is often the instrument that they use to actually accept the bid which the auctioneer offers. The auctioneer basically starts the bidding, asks for a bid from the room, offers the lot and if a person in the room wishes to accept that offer they either raise a hand or, if they obviously have a pre-arranged signal which is what often people think happens most of the time, they wink or touch their nose or scratch their head. But normally it's raising the catalogue or raising an arm just to say 'I accept that offer.'

I   And I have to ask you, has it ever happened that somebody really was scratching their head and not making a bid?

A   Yes, it ... it does happen but it's often a bit of a joke and the auctioneer knows very well that they're just waving to someone on the other side of the room and, for a bit of light relief, it's nice just to sort of make the point that you should definitely raise your catalogue if you actually wish to accept the bid.

I   So you give somebody a shock but it's not ... they don't have to go away with the goods afterwards?

A   I think it's very important and an auctioneer will always try and keep a little bit of entertainment going, because after all it can get terribly dull if you're just there and things are being sold and nothing else is happening. And one of the joys of an auction is that anything can happen, um, you get people getting what they call 'auction fever', which is basically getting slightly carried away, shall we say. You get a lot of excitement and one of the skills of an auctioneer is to control the room and to encourage that sort of relaxed but competitive atmosphere, and it's gimmicks like, um, asking the lady whether she was in fact bidding £500 when she's just come into the room to wave hello to her mother on the other side that makes it a little bit more interesting.

I   Has there been a really memorable sale in your mind, or an item which reached a really surprising price?

A   Yes, oh, very many. Um, I suppose as far as sales are concerned, one of the ... always the more interesting sales tend to be where you're selling up the contents of a large house when the family have moved or decided to move, specifically the sort of country house type. And they're the sales that always seem to encourage a lot of people to want to go and have a look around the house as well as the contents. They're always very well, er,

I   ... attended.

A   ... attended. And you can get some very big surprises in those sort of sales. I remember a painting which in fact we discovered in the coal hole of a very large house, just south of Bristol, which was in an appalling condition – you could hardly see what was actually underneath it – and we ended up by selling it for £3,500 ... um ... and that was really, we were hoping that it would get something around there, but it was a very speculative thing and it was nice to actually have got a very good price for it, which I think it was a very good price for it.

I   Yes ...

A   In the same auction, in fact, we had a very large bedroom suite, which we sold for £25,000, and again part of the suite was a four-poster bed and we found part of the four-poster bed in one of the outhouses, we found the uprights in the swimming pool and we found the rest of the bed literally scattered around in cupboards all round the house.

I Have you found that you've become very interested in a particular area of, well, antiques or collectibles or whatever, yourself?

A Um, yes, I mean, it's difficult because being what we call a provincial auctioneer, in other words, not being in a very large organisation I'm called upon to value items in a very broad sense. In other words, I have to do jewellery as well as rugs, pictures, furniture, right the way through, anything that you'd find in somebody's house, so I have to make sure that my interest, shall we say, is generalist. My personal taste, I suppose, tends to follow that interest. I wouldn't be doing what I'm doing after all if I'm doing it well, unless I was interested in it, and I suppose my ... I prefer ... I like furniture, I like wood, I like the feel of wood and I like the look of wood and I very much admire the craftsmanship that you get in wood. That is probably my preference. One of the problems of being an auctioneer is that you tend to see items which you would like to own but you can't afford. And because you see the nice items, you don't really want to own the items which you can afford so you're in a bit of a cleft stick, but that's life.

I One last question ... if you had to give advice to somebody who had never been to an auction but wanted to, what would you say?

A Don't be scared and do it. It's much easier to bid at an auction than you think and I think it's exciting. If you're bored by walking round a supermarket or going to a shop, go to an auction and I think it will change your attitude on the way that items can be bought and sold. Go and try it.

I Fine. Thank you very much.

UNIT 6B

▶Focus on listening 1 (p. 167)

A = Presenter   B = Brian Collins   C = William Rudd
D = Patricia Pole   E = Graham Clarke

A Unfortunately redundancy is a fact of life in Britain these days. And whether you work for a big multi-national company, or a small family firm, it can happen to anyone. Thousands of people have lost their jobs through redundancy in recent years. But with each lost job, there is the so-called 'golden handshake'. What do people do with this money? Do they spend it all on luxuries? Invest it? Or use it to start their own small businesses? We report on four cases of people who used their redundancy money to change their lives.

Brian Collins is 34. Until he was in his late twenties, he had a well-paid, responsible job in the electrical industry. But he suddenly realised that he could be worried to death by the time he was 30. Then, when he was offered a job in Scotland teaching sailing, he decided to take the opportunity to do something completely different. Four years later, however, the firm he was working for got into difficulties and Brian was made redundant.

B I spent the £350 I received in redundancy money on a holiday in Tenerife! And while I was there, I lay on the beach in the sun wondering what on earth I was going to do. In the end, I decided to go back to Scotland and start my own boat repair firm.

A Brian didn't expect to make much money from boat repairs, and at first he needed the £40 a week he received in a government grant. Now, eight months later, his income is £20,000 – much more than he would he earning in industry. And he enjoys working for himself.

B Yes, I'm much happier than I was when I was working for someone else, and I've had fewer sleepless nights this year than I did last year when I was worried about whether I might upset the boss!

A William Rudd is 54 now. He worked for a multi-national chemical company for 20 years until 1980 when he decided to take early retirement. He says he'd known for about a year that he was going to leave and he'd been applying for office jobs. When he didn't get anywhere, he decided to use his redundancy money of £70,000 to open a butcher's shop in central London. He started in July – the worst time for a butcher's shop like his, unfortunately, and his overdraft just kept going up.

C I managed to spend far too much money on doing the place up because I didn't want it to look too ordinary. It was all rather frightening because there was nobody between me and the bank manager! I don't know if what I did was brave or foolish – a bit of both, I suppose.

A But at the same time, William was enjoying himself. It was fun serving behind the counter in the shop – completely different from his previous job, and much harder work. And his business is going from strength to strength. In fact, he has just opened a second London shop.

A Patricia and Rex Pole are a married couple who both worked for a bank until they were made redundant three years ago. With their redundancy money they bought a public house on the south coast of England.

D The terms of the redundancy payment were based on the number of years you had worked in the bank. Between us we had done 33 years, so it was quite a good sum. It gave us approximately £30,000.

A In fact, a couple of years earlier, they had started thinking about going into the pub business. When they found a place they wanted to buy, they put all their redundancy money into it.

D If we'd known what it would be like, I don't think we would have done it. It was absolutely awful to start with. We didn't know anything about running a pub – although we thought we did! We'd never had to worry about paying bills before. And we ran the pub totally by ourselves which meant a seven-day week and terribly long hours. It was very physical work too, you're on your feet all the time and the first two months were very very hard. We hardly spoke to each other. Actually we were in a state of shock!

A   After 14 months, they decided to sell.

D   We realised we couldn't imagine spending the rest of our lives doing that kind of work. We wanted to have a private life again!

A   Patricia and Rex Pole have now returned to work in banking but they're glad to have tried the experiment.

A   Finally, we have Graham Clarke who is 57. He worked for 27 years as a salesman in Colchester.

E   I actually asked to be made redundant because I could see that things weren't going very well for the company. My rounds were getting smaller and smaller, and more branches were closing down.

A   He was made redundant in February and received £2,000 in redundancy pay.

E   I started working on the idea of becoming a magician because magic has been my hobby for nearly 40 years. I thought 'I've got a good collection of tricks, so I might as well see if I can make a living out of magic.'

A   He started his business in July under the name of Graham Clarke Magic, and the first step was to contact agents and to advertise in the local newspaper. He was also interviewed on local radio.

E   I don't expect to make any money for at least a year because you need to spend at least a third of your income on advertising. I'll know how I stand by next January and then, if things are going well, it'll still take another year to eighteen months to start to establish the business properly.

A   Graham has already worked at a number of children's parties and he plans to do after-dinner acts as well. He is hoping to be able to work all over the country and even abroad and we wish him, and everyone else who has proved there can be life after redundancy, well.

▶ Focus on listening 2 (p. 173)

A = Interviewer   B = John

A   John, when we talked last time you told me about your long career in the Merchant Navy. That lasted for …?

B   It lasted for … 12 years, in all.

A   And you said it was your friends who finally persuaded you to make the break and leave.

B   Yes.

A   Well, after that I know you started a completely new career in a hospital, working as a male nurse. Tell me how that came about.

B   I was in hospital for about six weeks, and while I was there I was thinking what to do. I absolutely didn't want to go back in the Merchant Navy. I'd actually got to the end of that then! I don't think that while I was in hospital I actually considered nursing as a possibility, but when I came out – it was very awkward. Because when I left the Merchant Navy I was 31, and pretty well untrained for anything, really. I mean, I could wait at table and mix cocktails and make crepes suzettes, and things – so I could have worked in a hotel, I suppose. But that would have been like leaving the Merchant Navy and starting to do more or less the same thing as what I'd been doing. But it would've been worse because the pay wouldn't have been so good. And there's not many things that you can actually train for when you're 31… And … um … God bless nursing because they'll take people up to the age of 50 provided they have the right educational qualifications. And it all suddenly became

very attractive. I remembered seeing the nurses work in hospital, and I thought 'I'd quite like to do that' and I had the right qualifications and they were very short of nurses at that time.

A   Where did you start?

B   I started where I finished – at Frenchay Hospital in Bristol. I went for an interview there and I knew immediately that it was a nice place to work. And I never left it.

B   So they accepted you?

B   They accepted me, believe it or not!

A   How long was the training?

B   Three years, initially. I did three years general nurse training, and then I did two years training in mental illness. And it was marvellous!

A   Were you trained as a male nurse, or just as … a nurse?

B   There is really no difference. When I started, there were seven other men in the group I was in. Now, compared with today, that's very high. Because today you might get one man in a class of twenty. So there were a lot coming into the profession then.

A   What were the hours then?

B   Forty hours a week.

A   Is that the same now?

B   It's 37½ now.

A   And how did the pay compare with being in the Merchant Navy?

B   The pay was very low compared with the Merchant Navy. It was very difficult to live on. During the three years that I … that I did nurse training, I spent almost all my own savings.

A   Were most people who did that training in their teens?

B   Oh yes.

A   And were they living at home?

B   Some were. Some were living in the nurses' home. The nurses' pay was reasonable if you lived in the nurses' home and ate at the hospital. But obviously, as a 31 year old, I didn't want to be living in the nurses' home. And when I found – even though it was a very small place to live – it was impossible not to dip into savings.

A   And did you ever question whether you were doing the right thing?

B   Oh no, never! It was the most marvellous time. In fact the training was the best part of the nursing. I've never enjoyed any of it as much as I enjoyed the three years' training.

A   Why was that?

B   Well, when you're a student, for one thing, you're having new experiences all the time. So that, once you've trained, and you take on a post in a ward, it becomes very routine. When you're a student, you do two months on an orthopaedic ward, and then you go for a month on a children's ward, then you go into the operating theatre for two months. So there's constant change. And it was a bit like being in the Merchant Navy because … instead of travelling from country to country, I was moving from ward to ward!

A   So how did you go from that into nurse teaching?

B   I think I got into teaching because I wanted to go on learning, while I was on the ward, so I did other courses as well as the basic training. And it was the next logical step. I remember my tutor saying 'Well, now you've got the Diploma of Nursing, and you've done all that you can do, have you ever thought about teaching?' Because they've always been very short of nurse teachers. They're always looking for nurse teachers.

A   Is that because there aren't many people who can teach?

B   Oh, I don't think being able to teach has got much to do with being a nurse teacher! It's very easy to say why they've always been short of nurse teachers. Because nurse teachers are paid exactly the same as ordinary nurses and you have to do all the extra work yourself without any extra pay. Anyway, I went away for a year and did a Certificate of Education.

A   And was it worthwhile?

B   Oh yes! I really enjoyed it. It was very very good to be away and to spend all your spare time studying.

A Do you regret at all that you didn't start nursing much earlier?

B No. I have no regrets in my life whatsoever. Even the bad things I don't regret. And I certainly don't regret spending my formative years going round the world. I don't think that I could ever have had anything to equal that, had I stayed on at school. Because I virtually went everywhere and saw an awful lot, and I don't think I'd have got that any other way. If I'd gone straight into nursing, I'd probably have got bored with it by now.